Anne Manera's Colorist's Color Palettes

A Reference Guide to Picking Colors for Coloring Pages

By Anne Manera

Copyright © 2019 Anne Manera
All rights reserved. No part of this publication may be reproduced, stored in a retrieval system, or transmitted, in any form or by any means, electronic, mechanical, photocopying, recording or otherwise, without prior written permission from the author.
ISBN: 9781799151685

Introduction

Use this book as your reference guide in choosing colors for your coloring page, painting, interior home project and more! Anne Manera, professional artist, illustrator and art instructor has compiled this reference book to assist your next coloring project.

Filled with reference guides including

- 30 Color Palettes
- 56 Color Schemes
- Color Wheel
- Warm & Cool Colors Chart
- Primary Colors Chart
- Secondary Colors Chart
- Complementary Colors Chart
- Analogous Colors Chart

Color Wheel

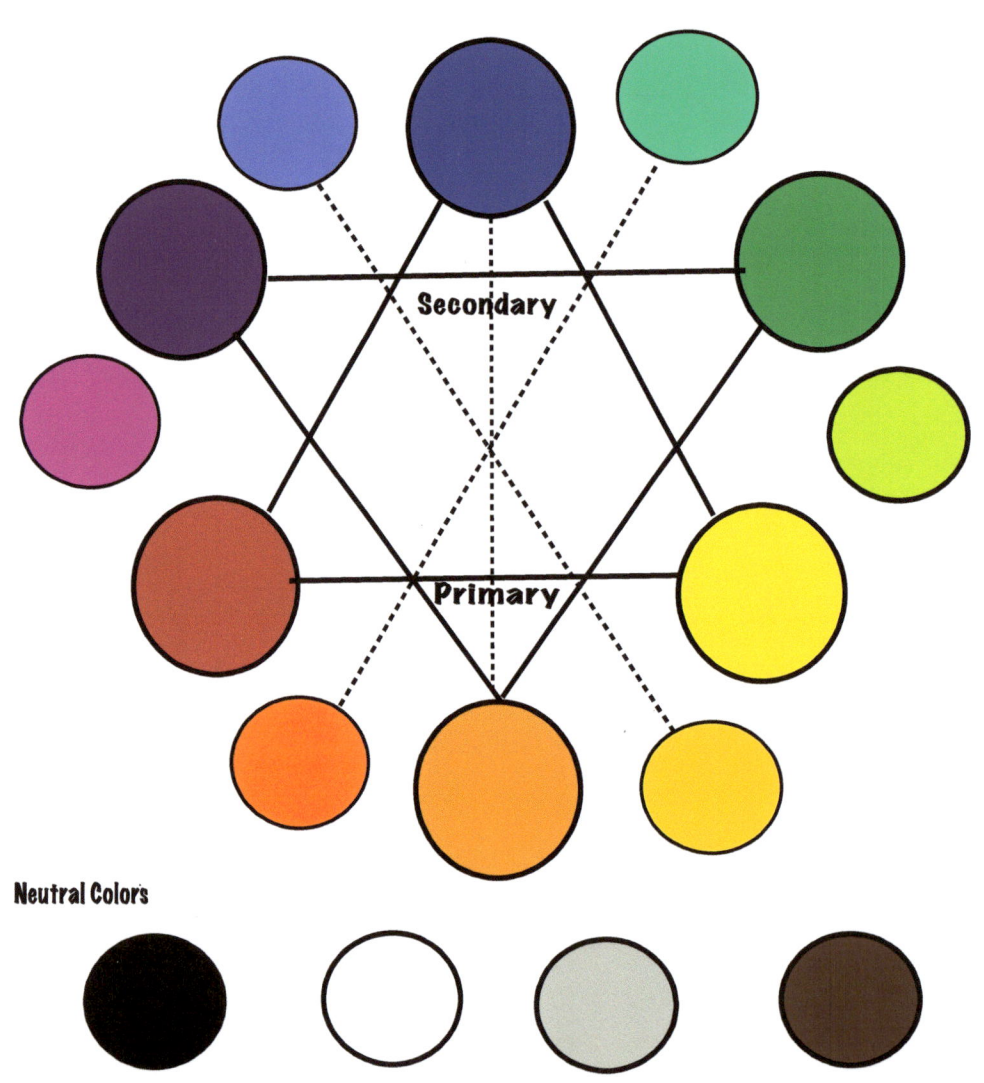

Neutral Colors

Primary Colors -
Colors that be created by mixing are Red, Yellow, Blue
Secondary Colors -
Colors that are made by mixing 2 Primary colors are Orange, Purple and Green
Analogous Colors -
Colors that are next to each other on the color wheel
Complementary Colors -
Colors that are across from one another on the color wheel

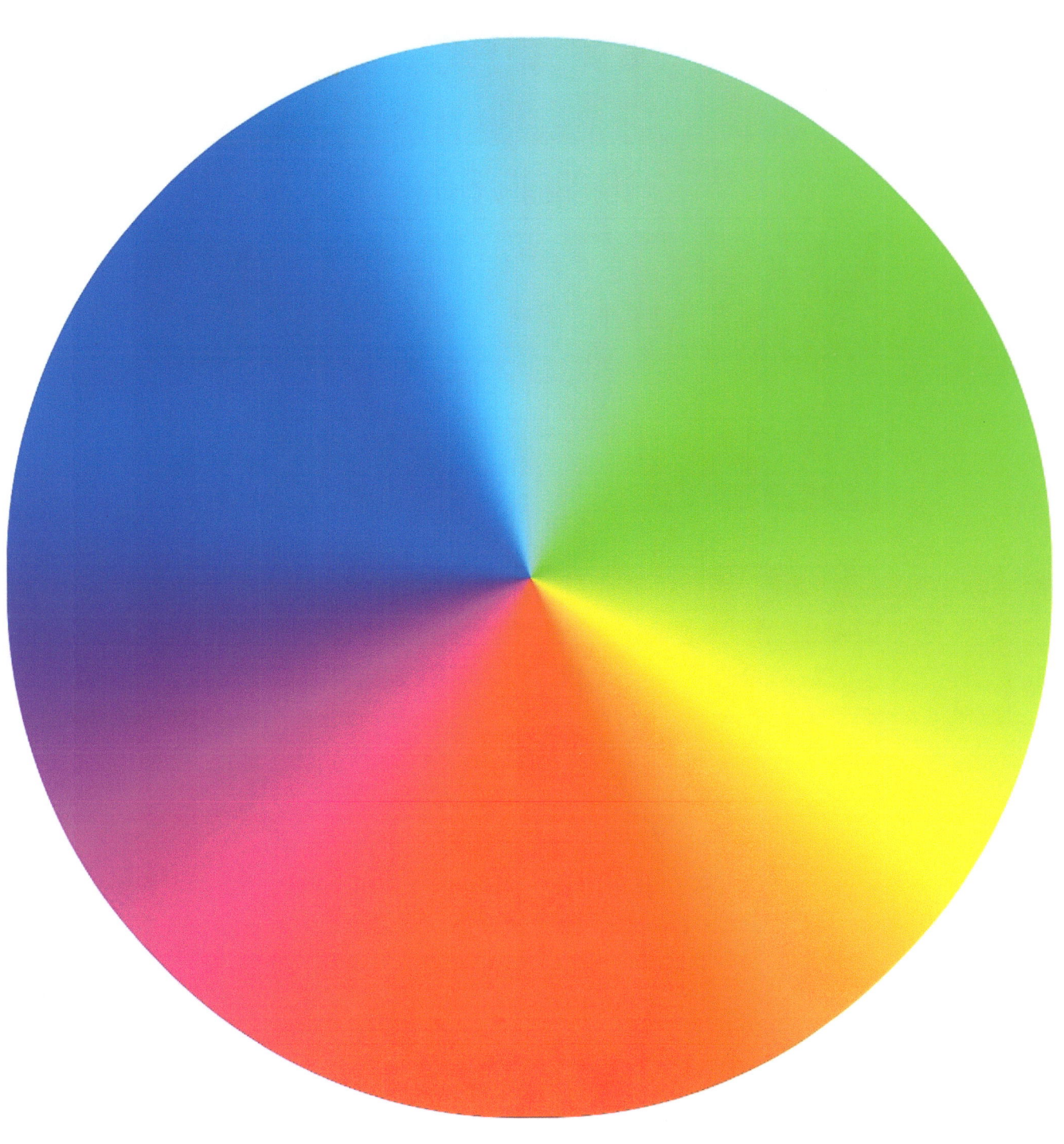

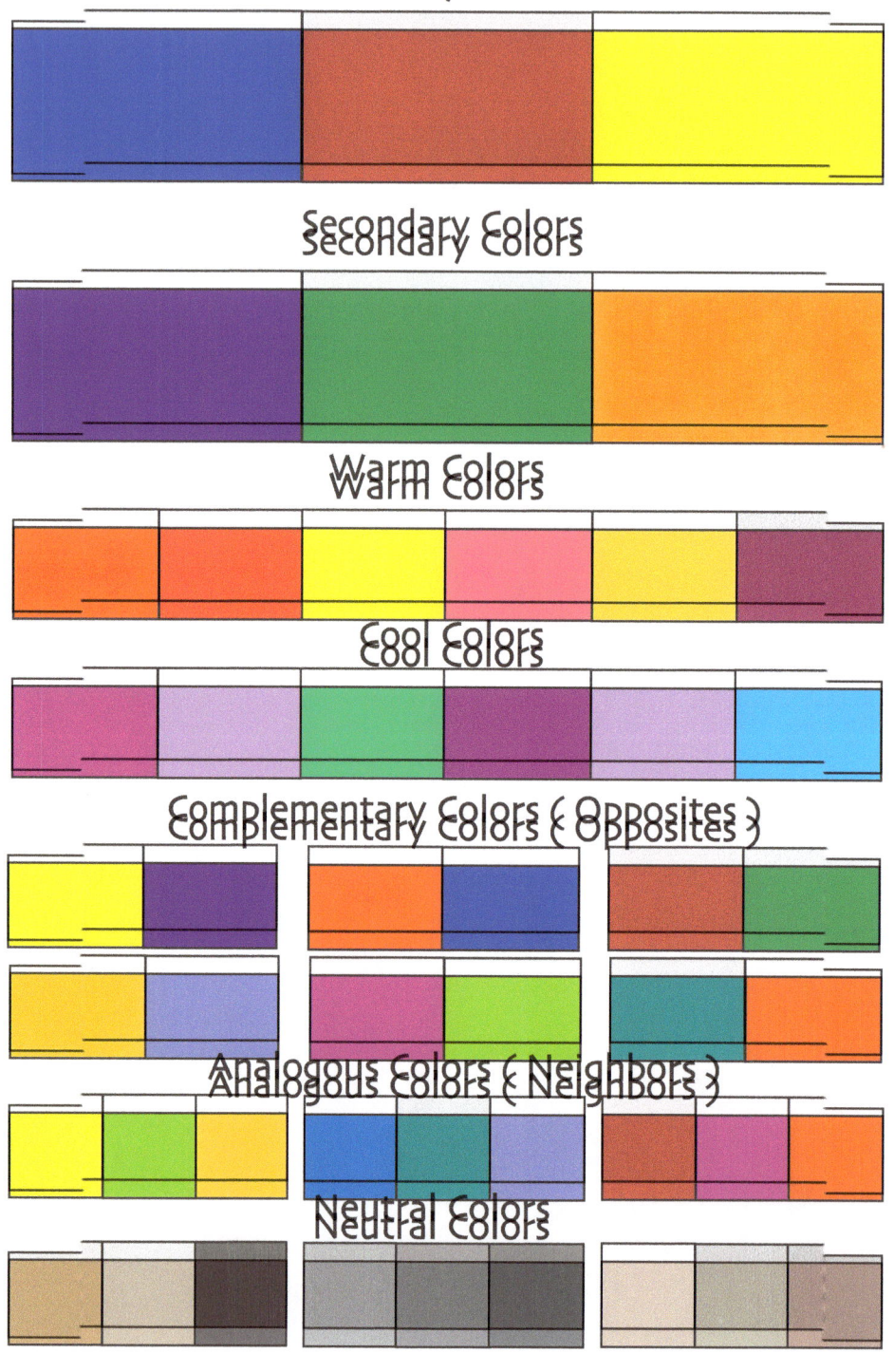

Color Schemes

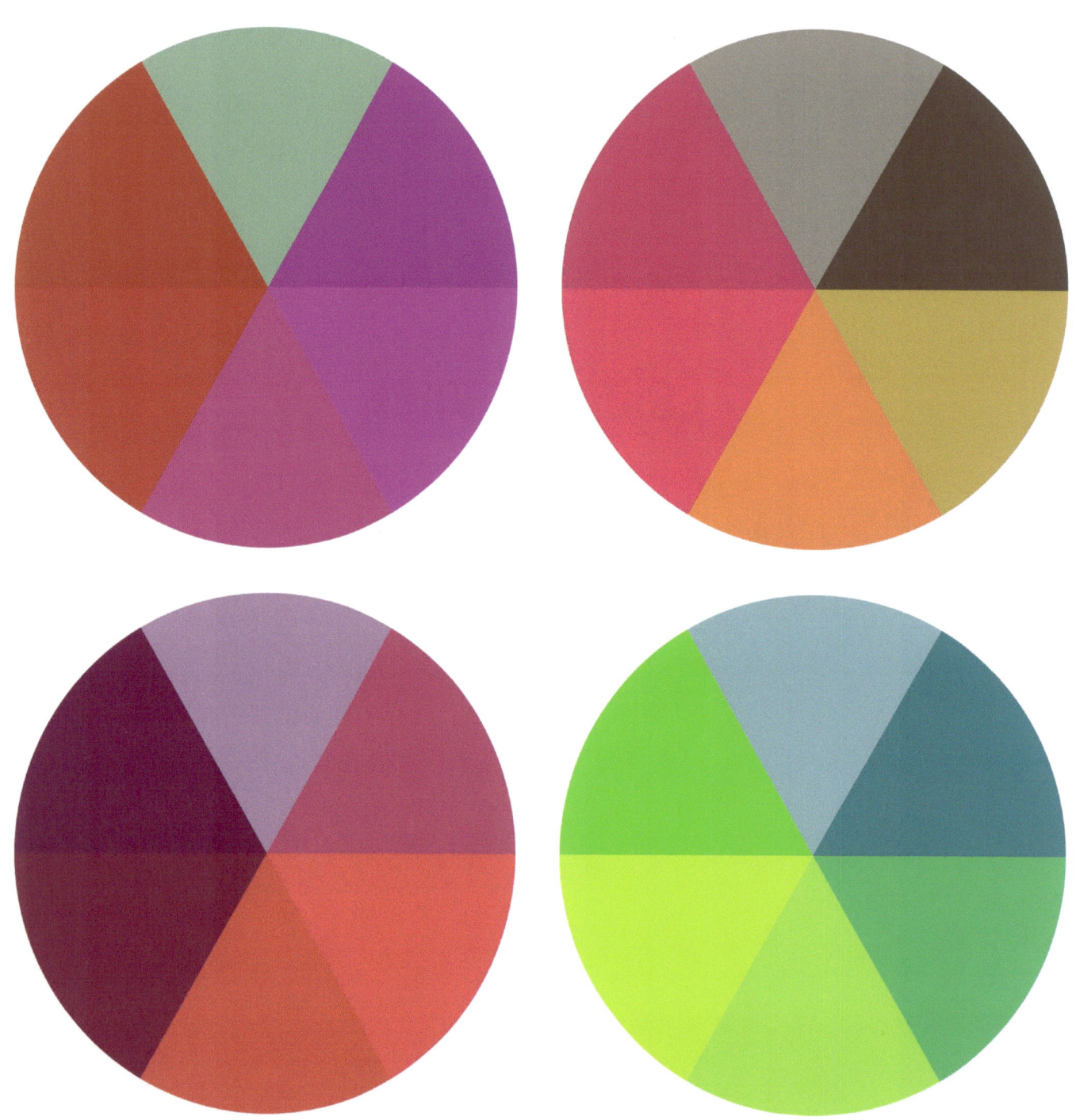

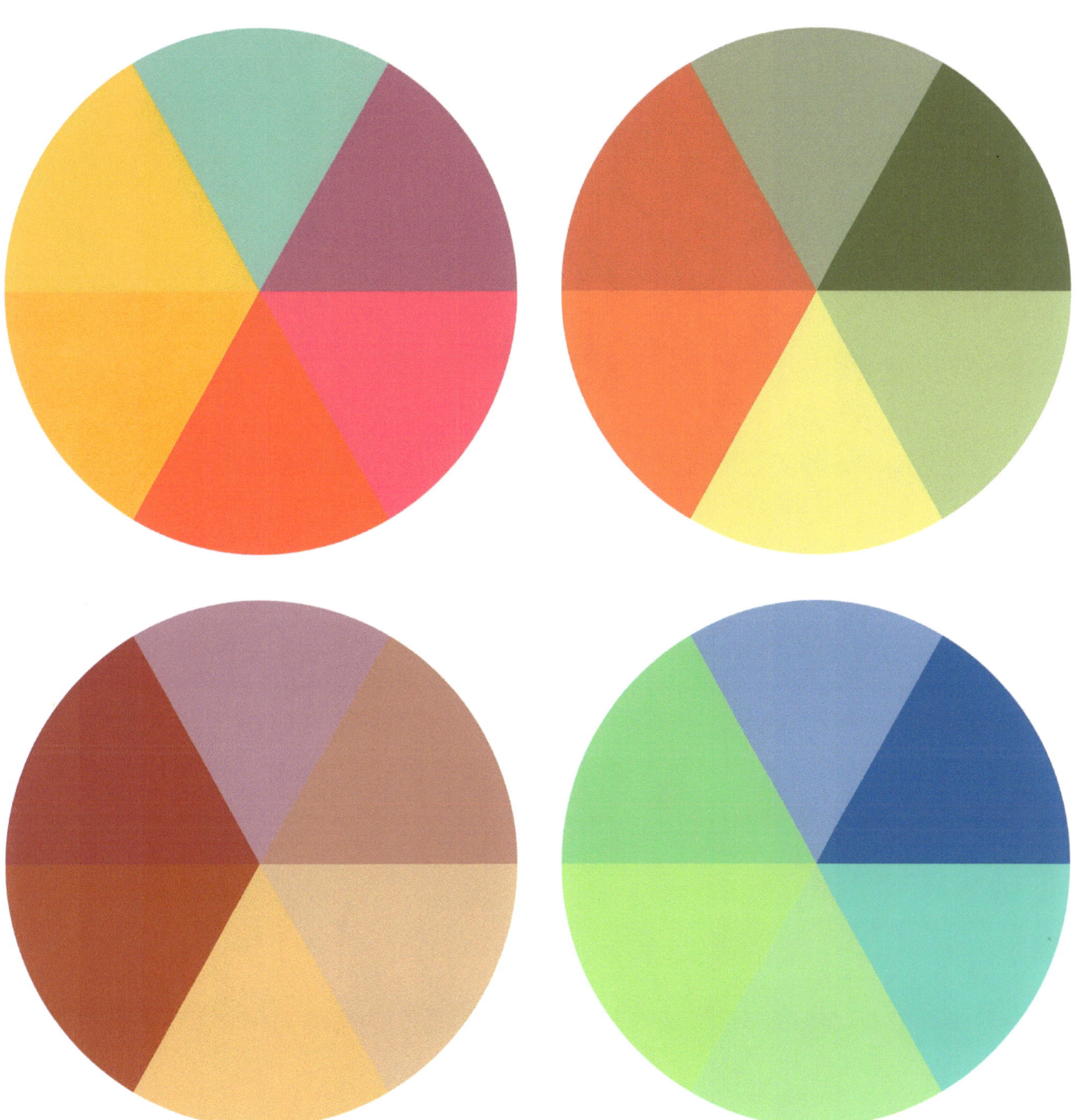

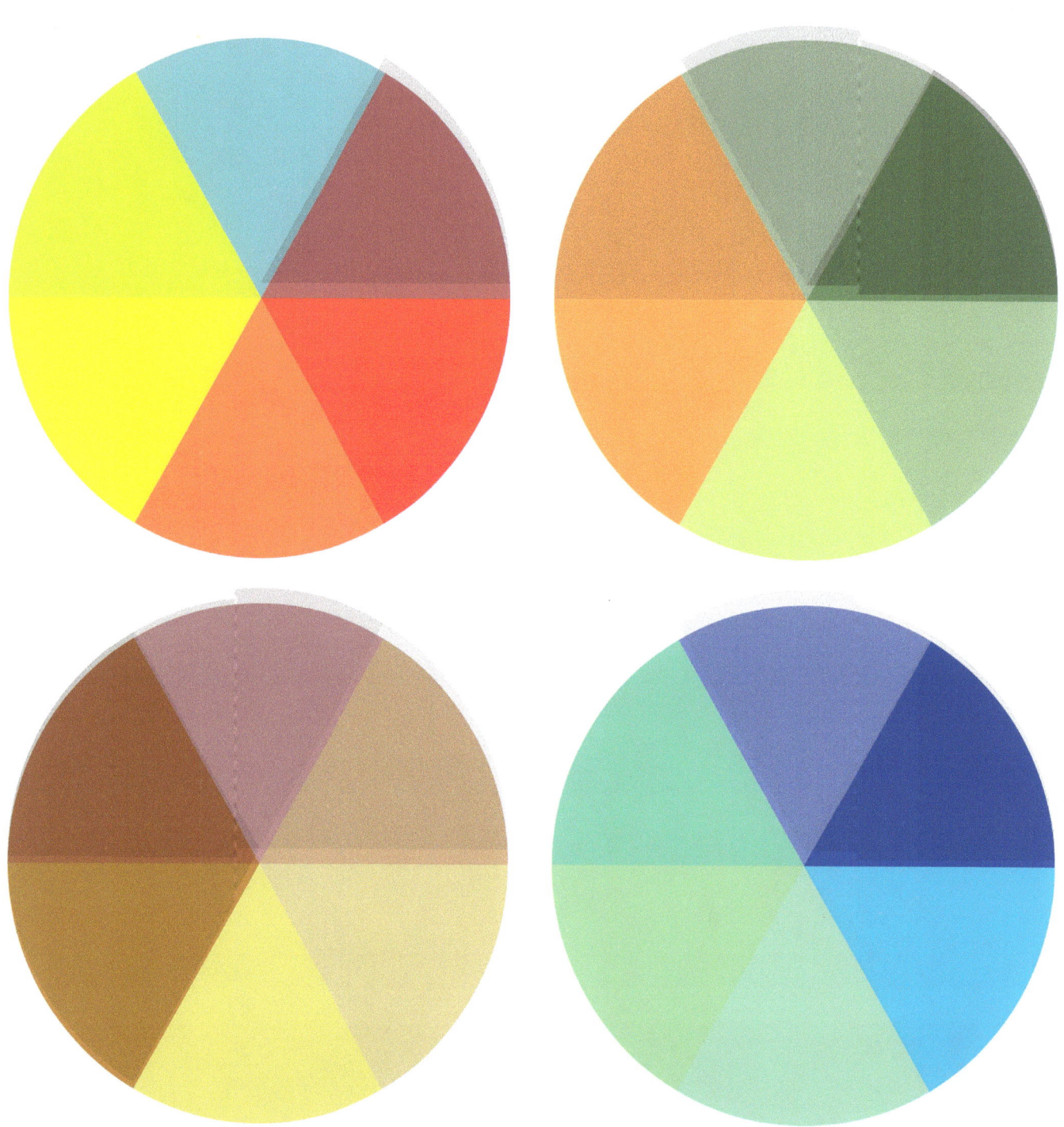

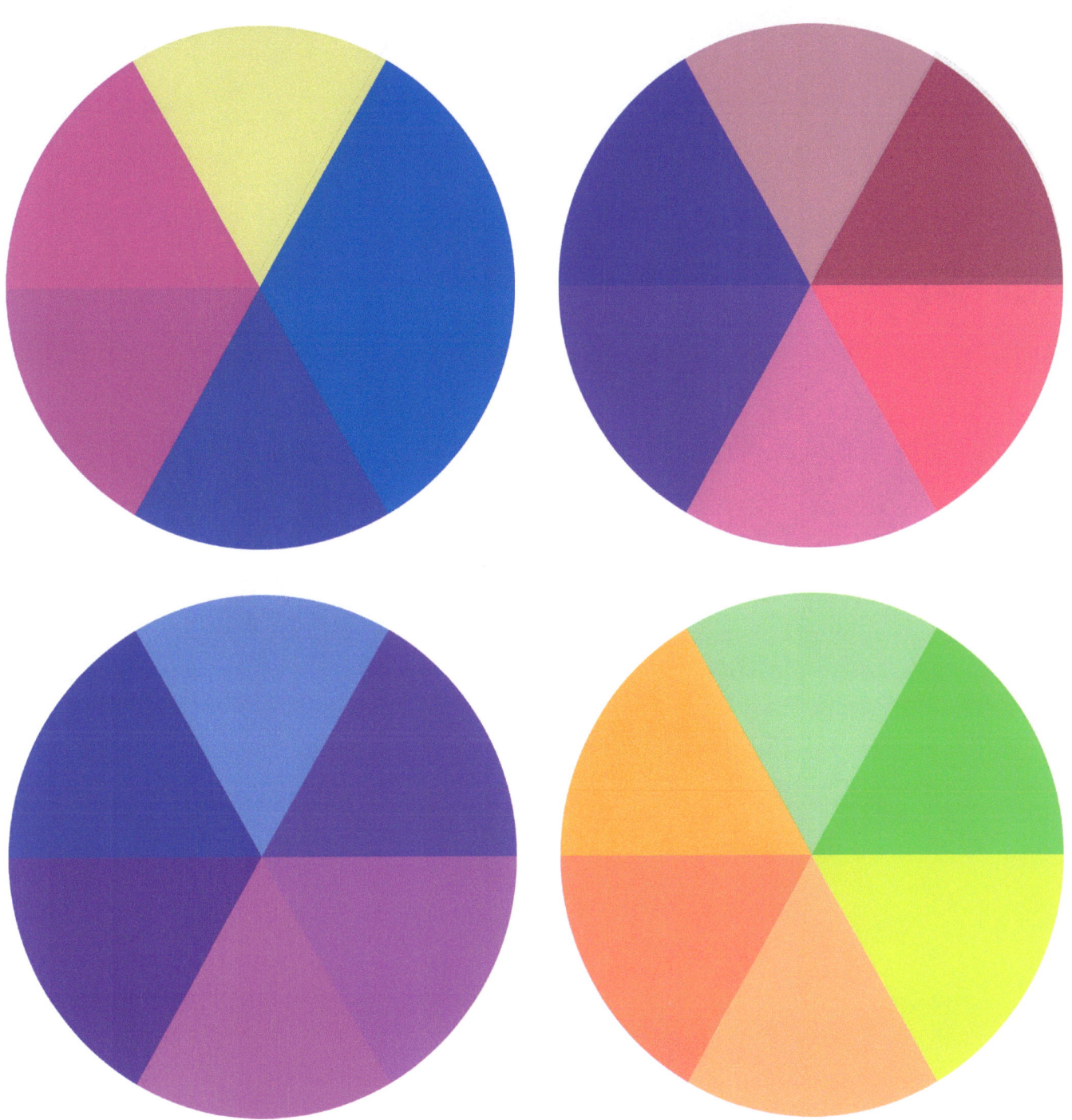

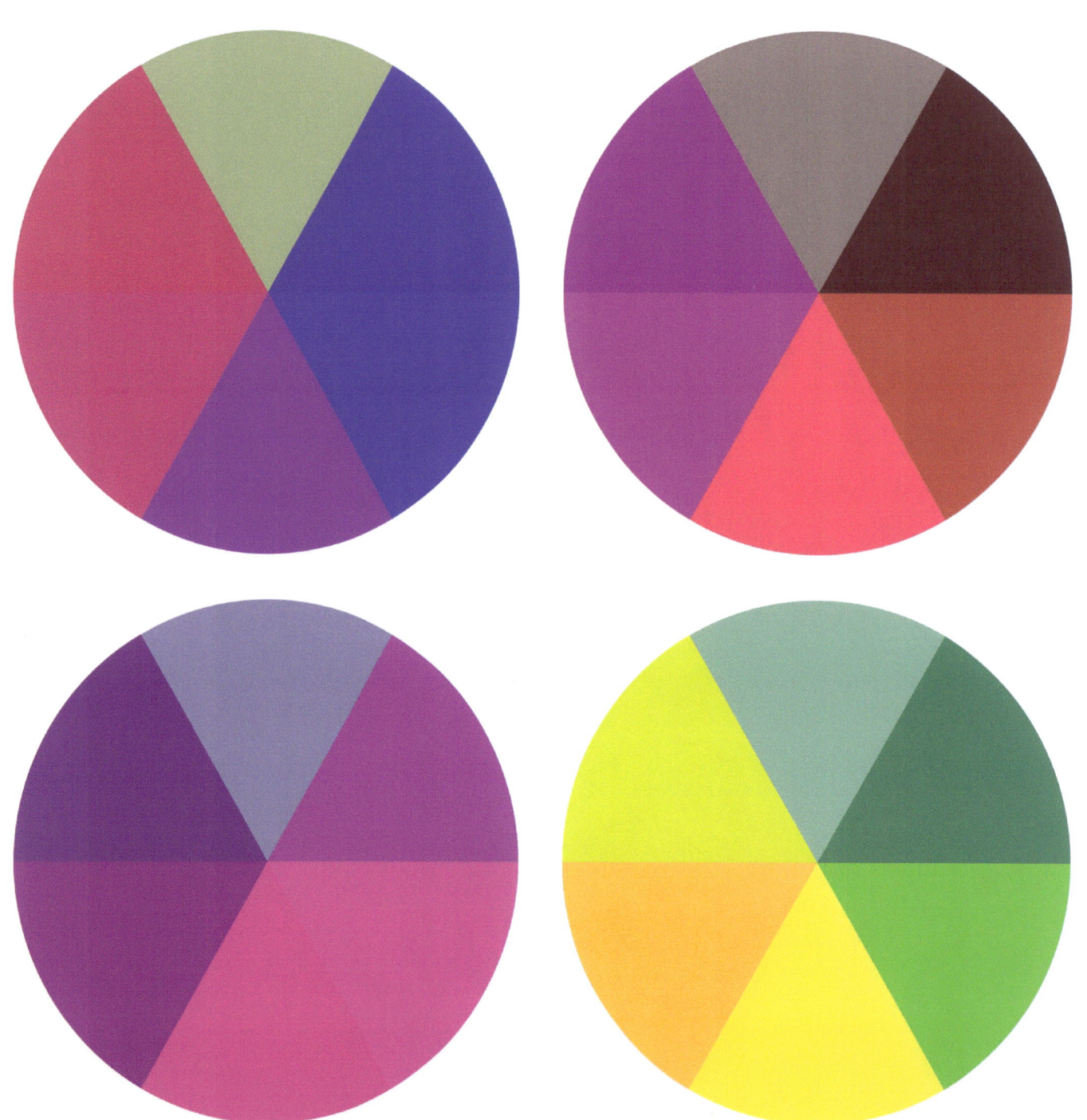

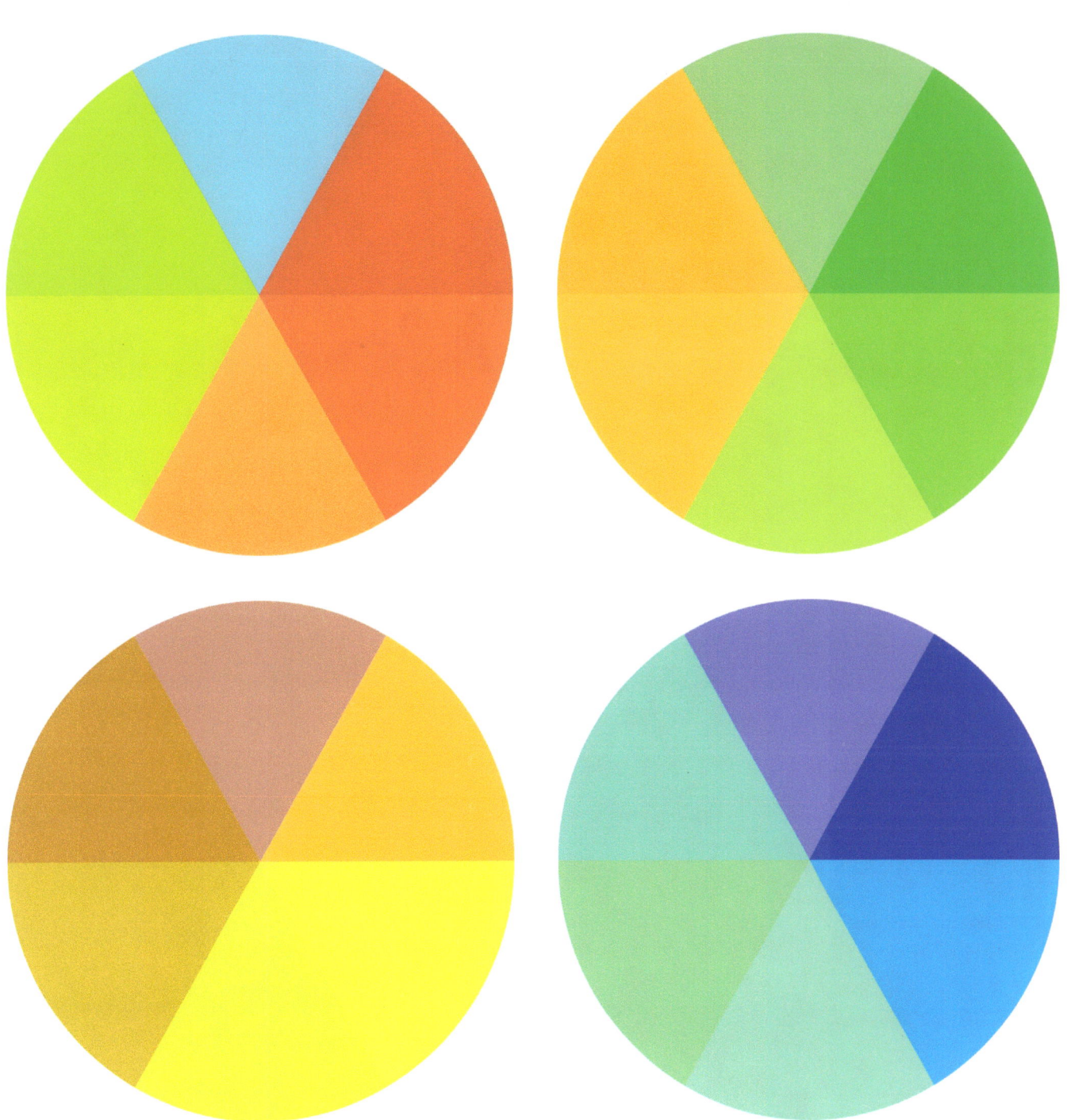

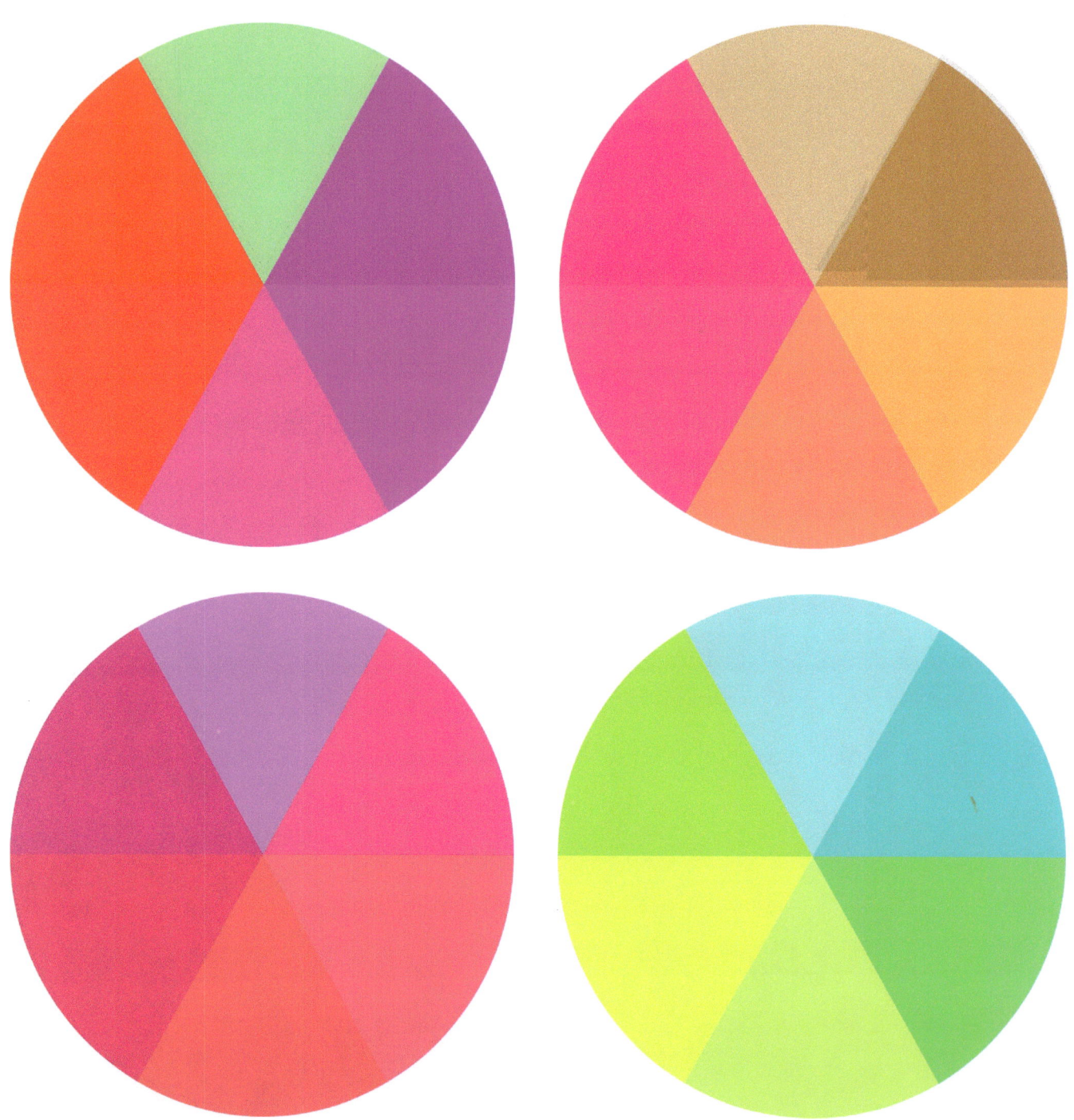

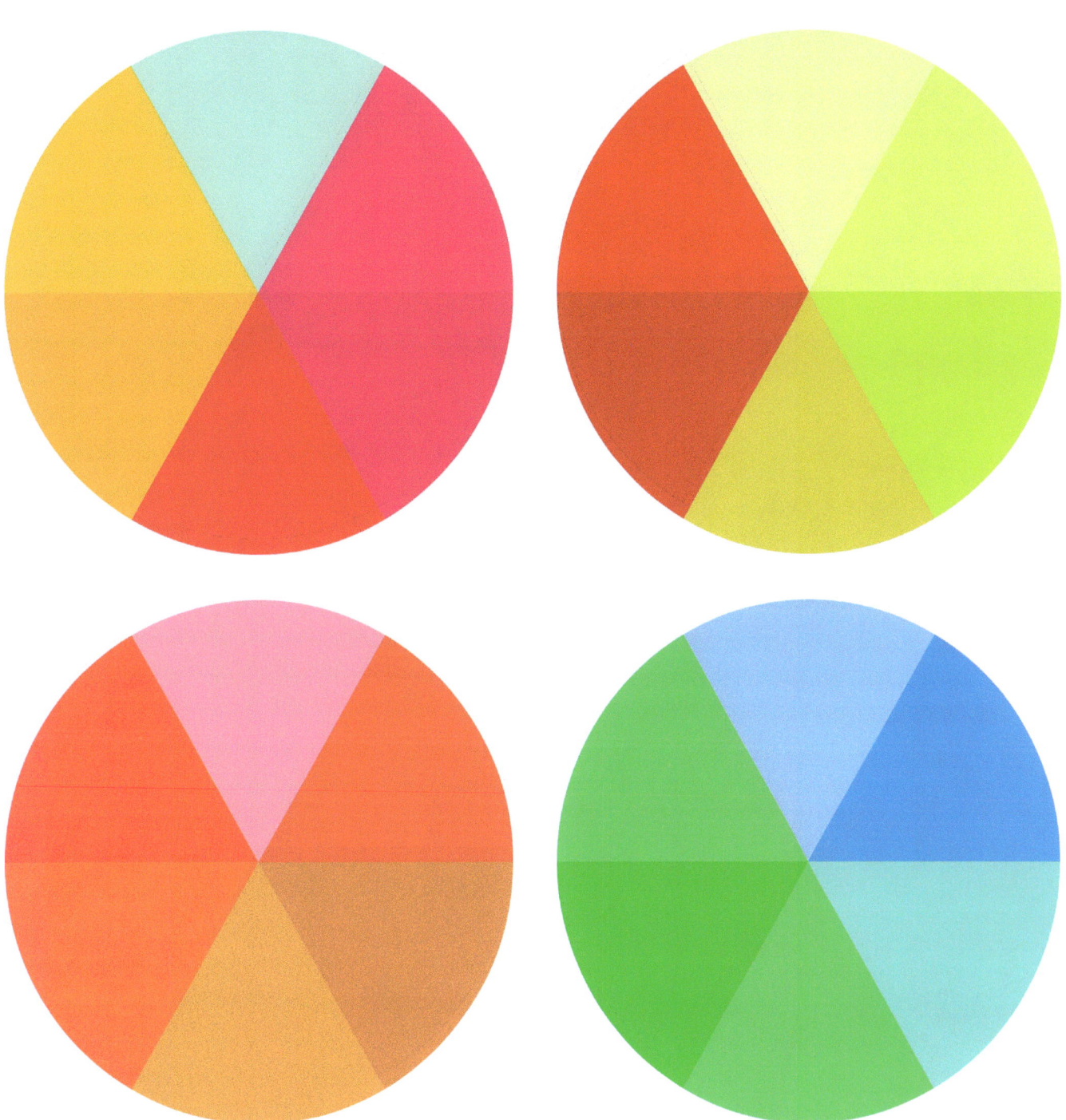

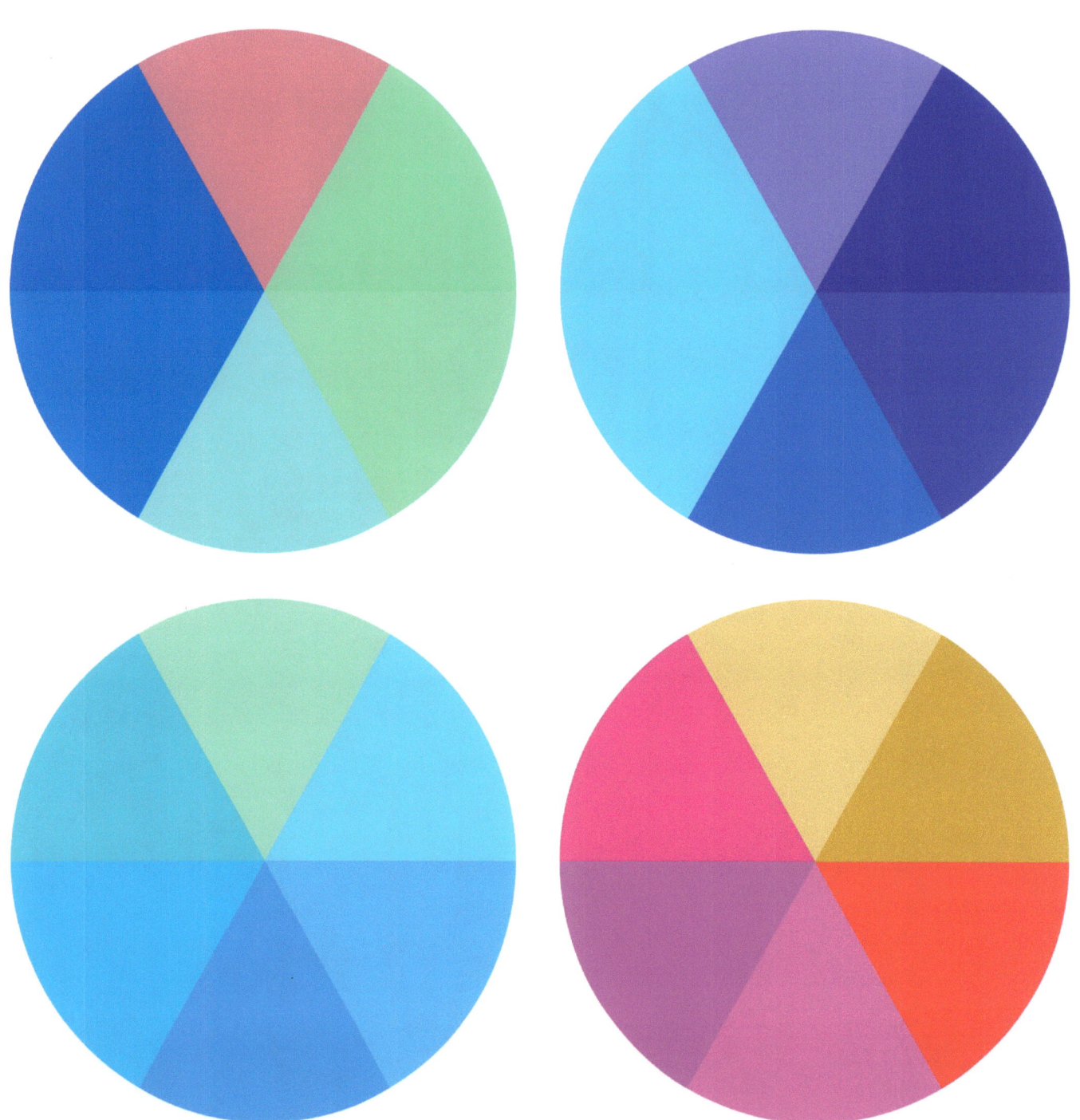

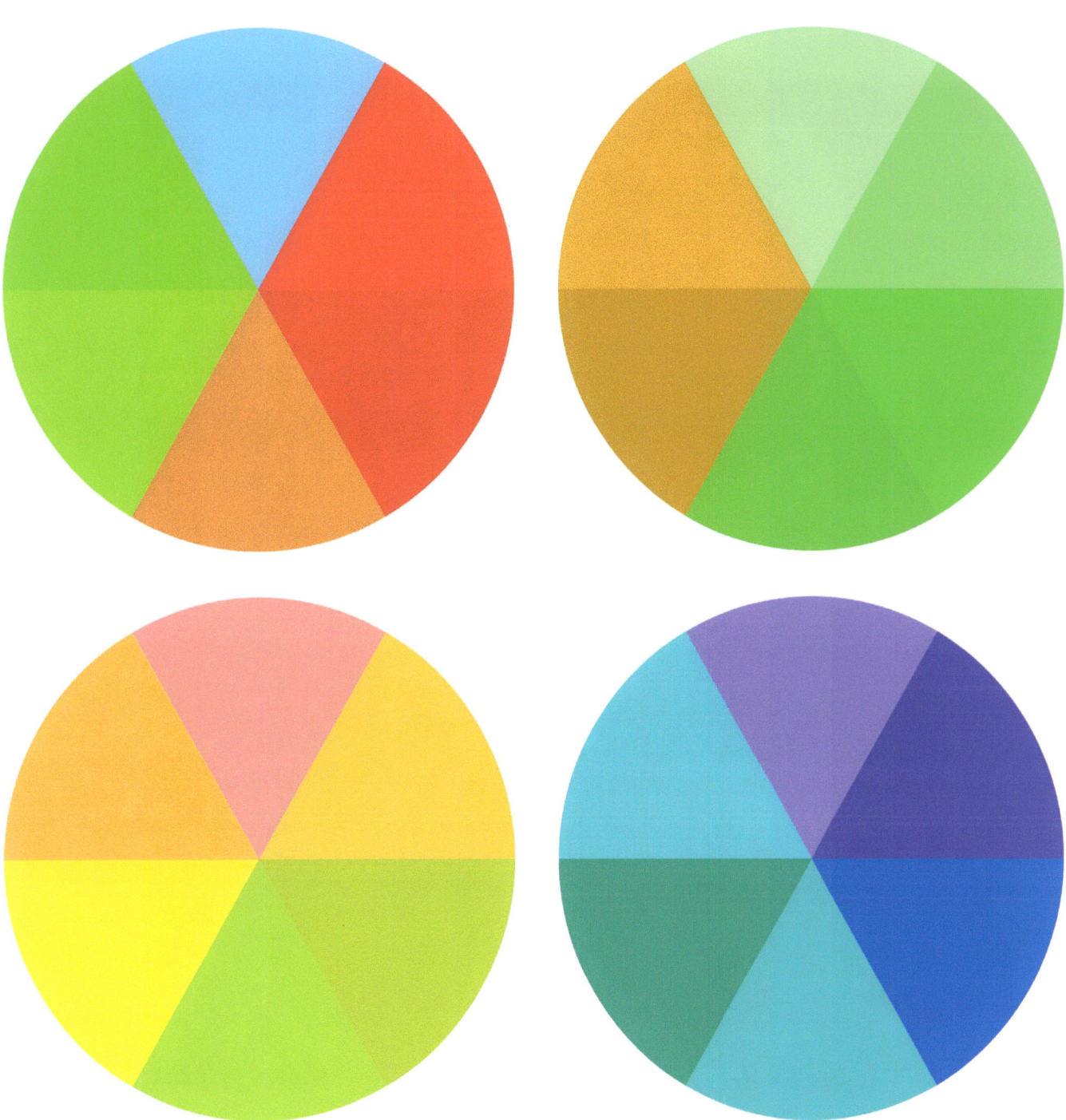

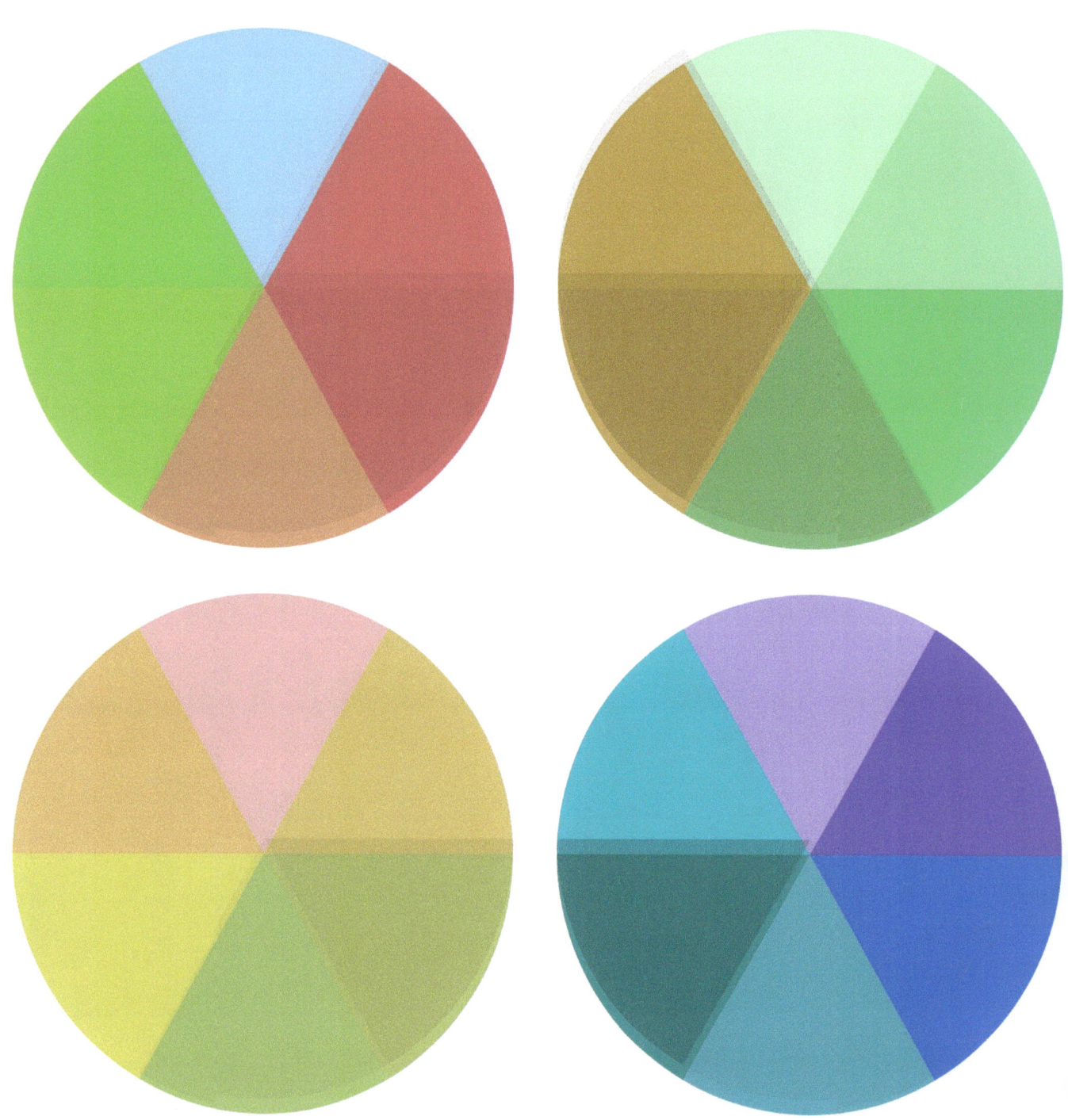

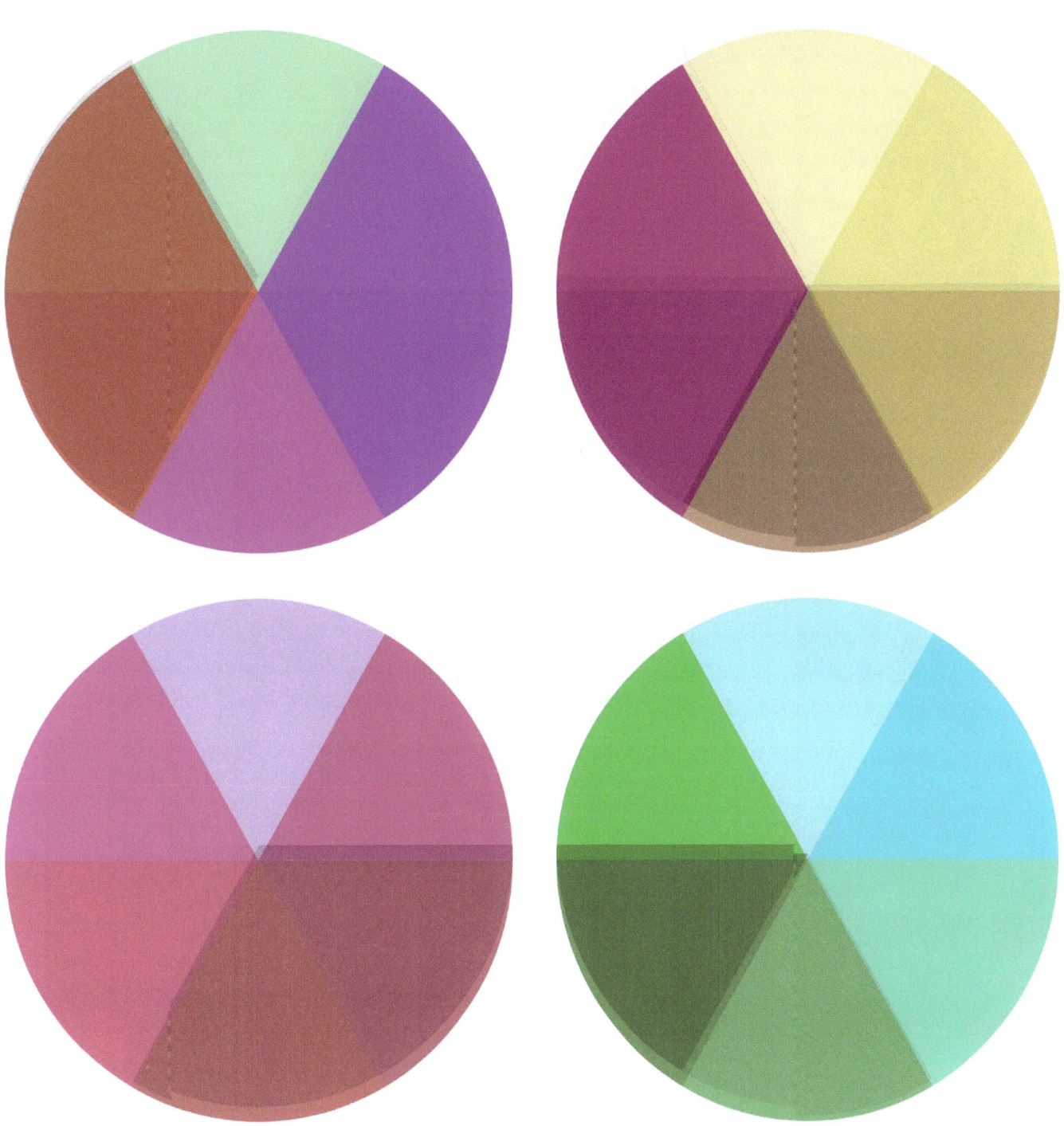

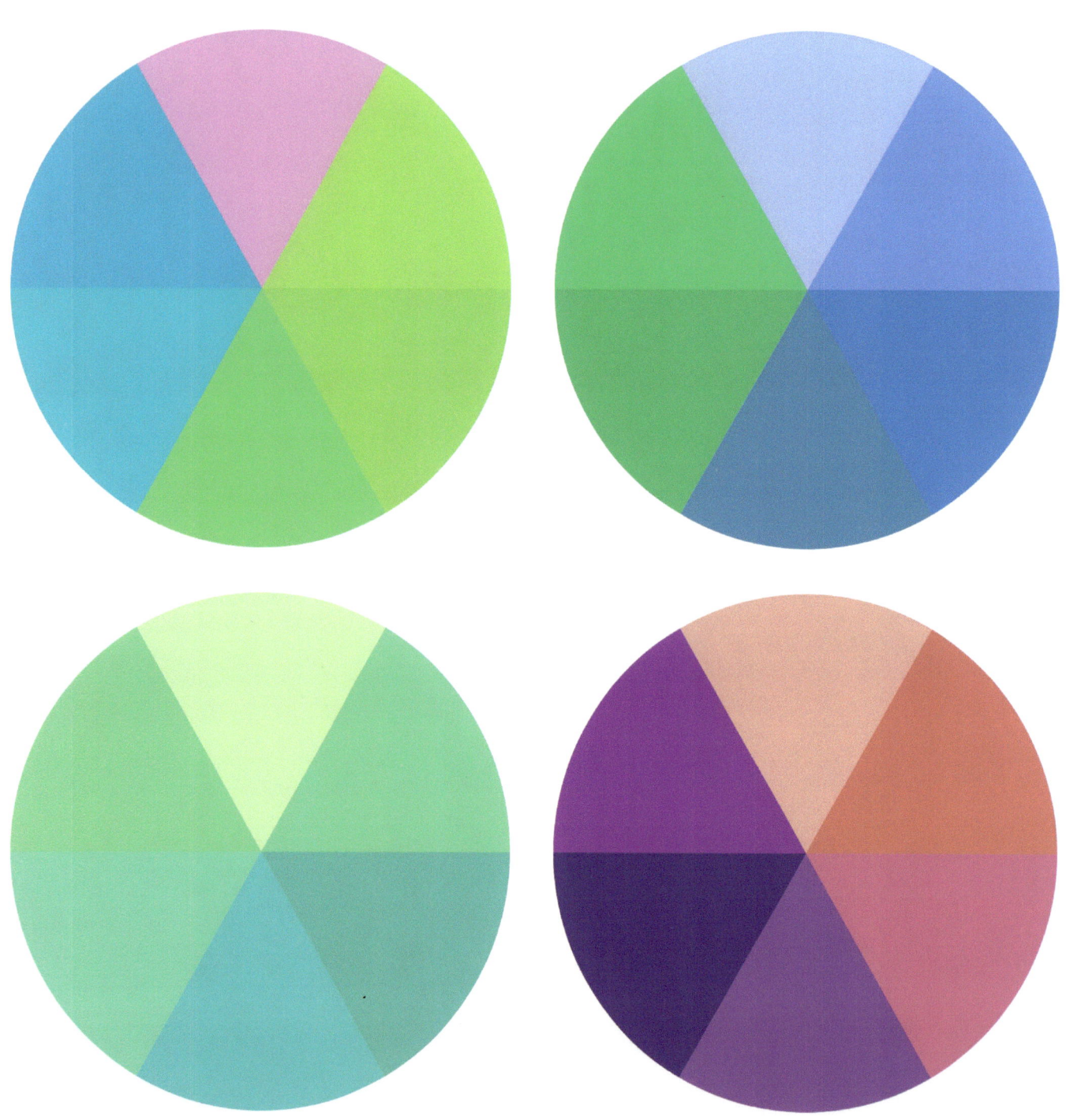

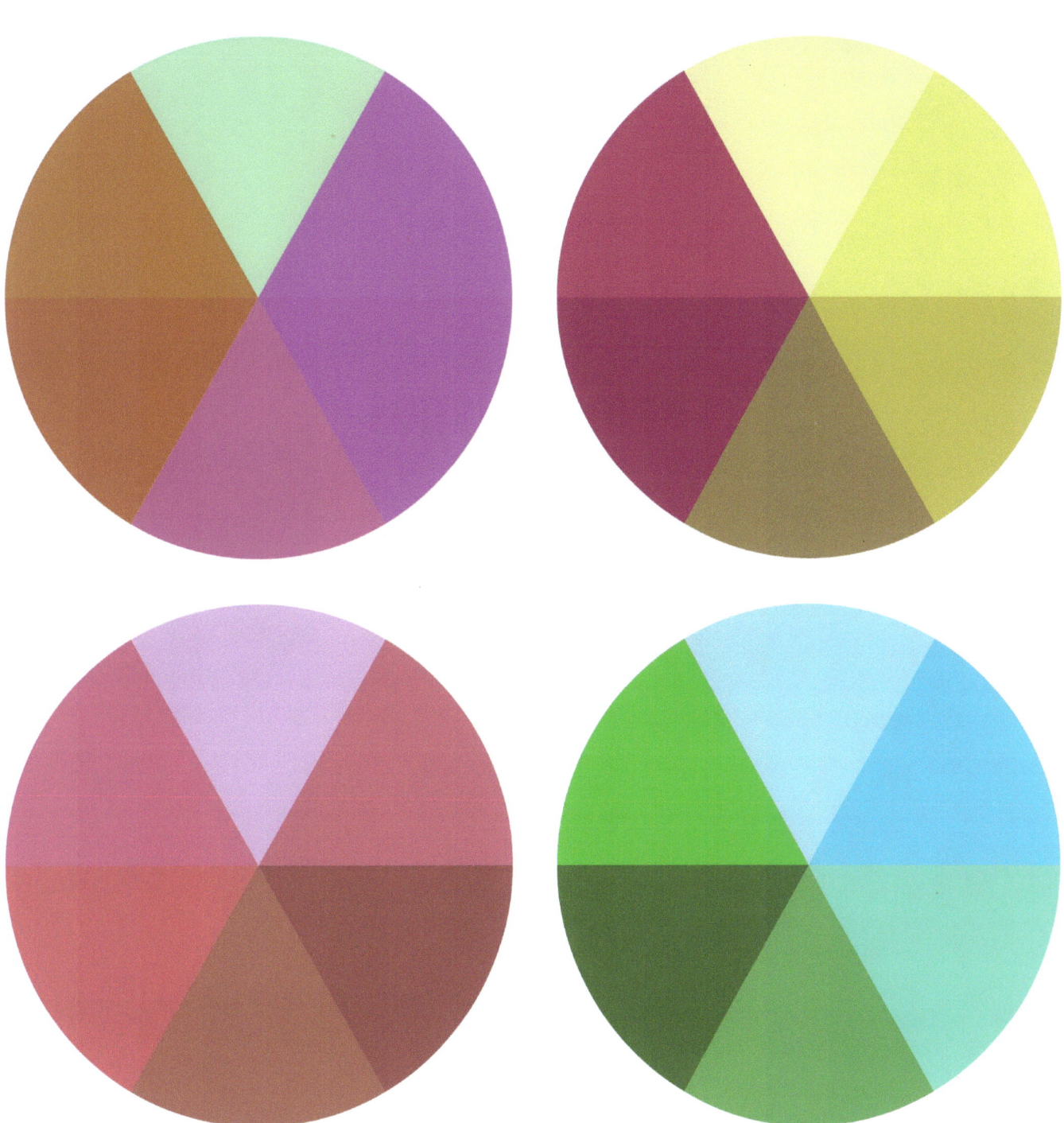

Color Palettes

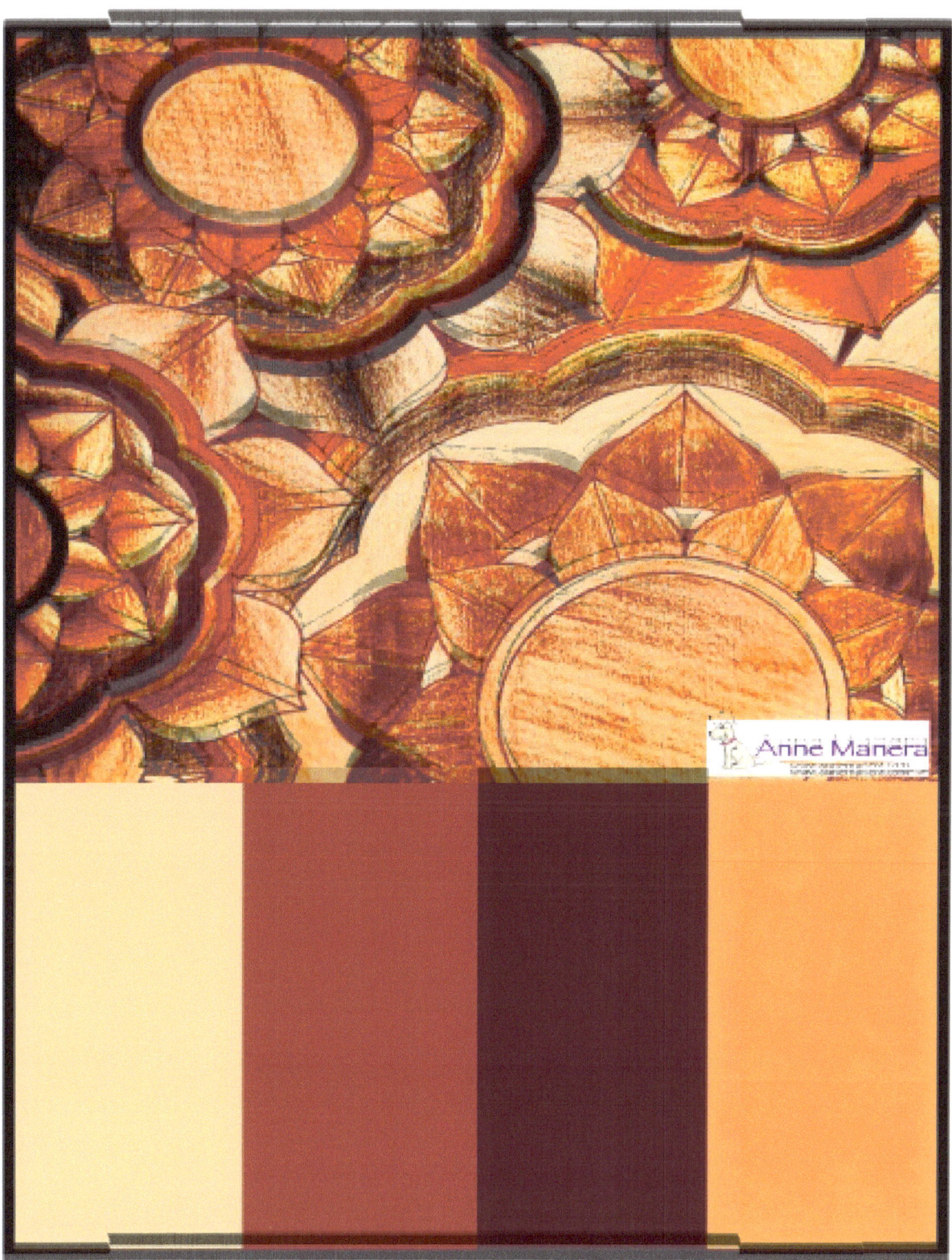

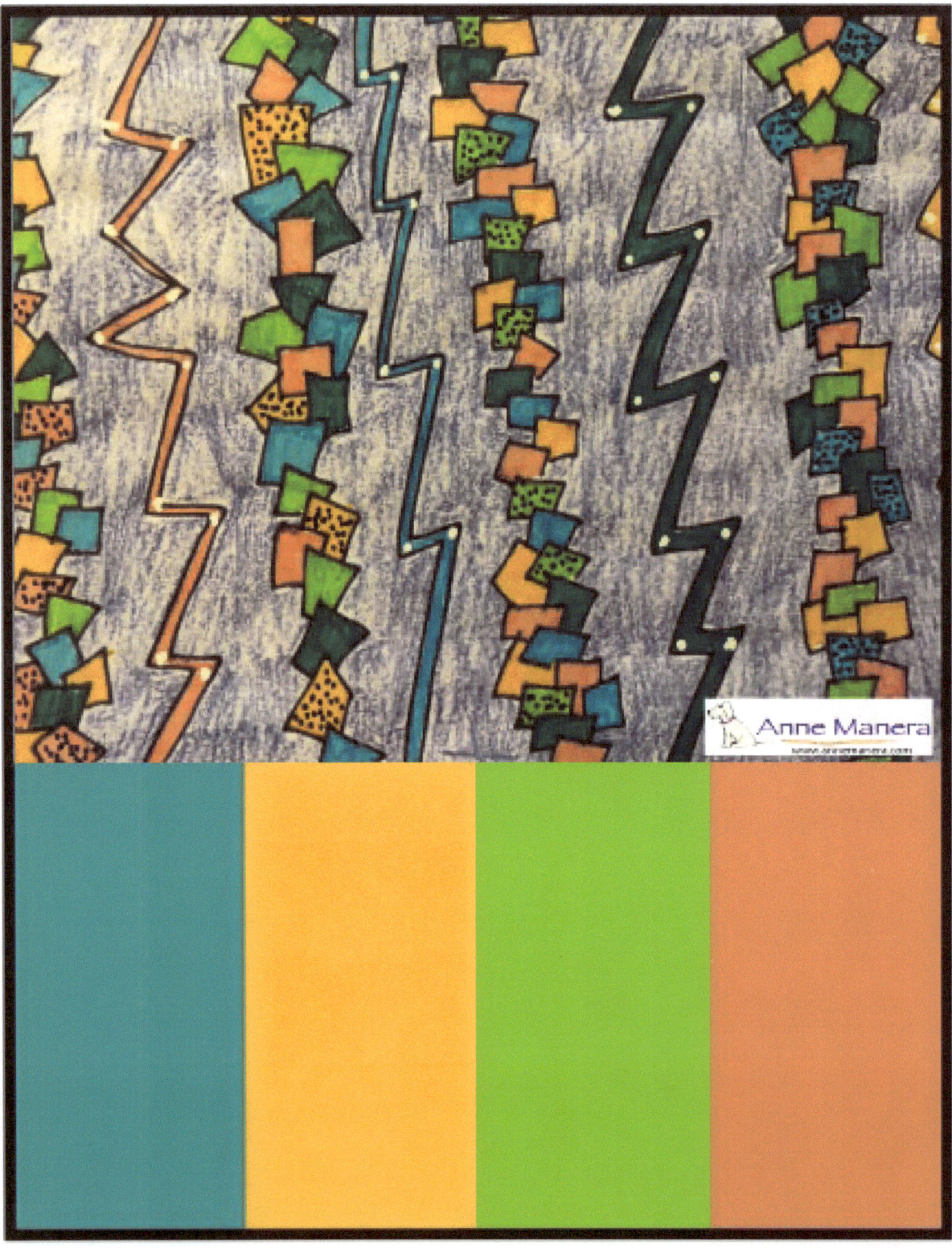

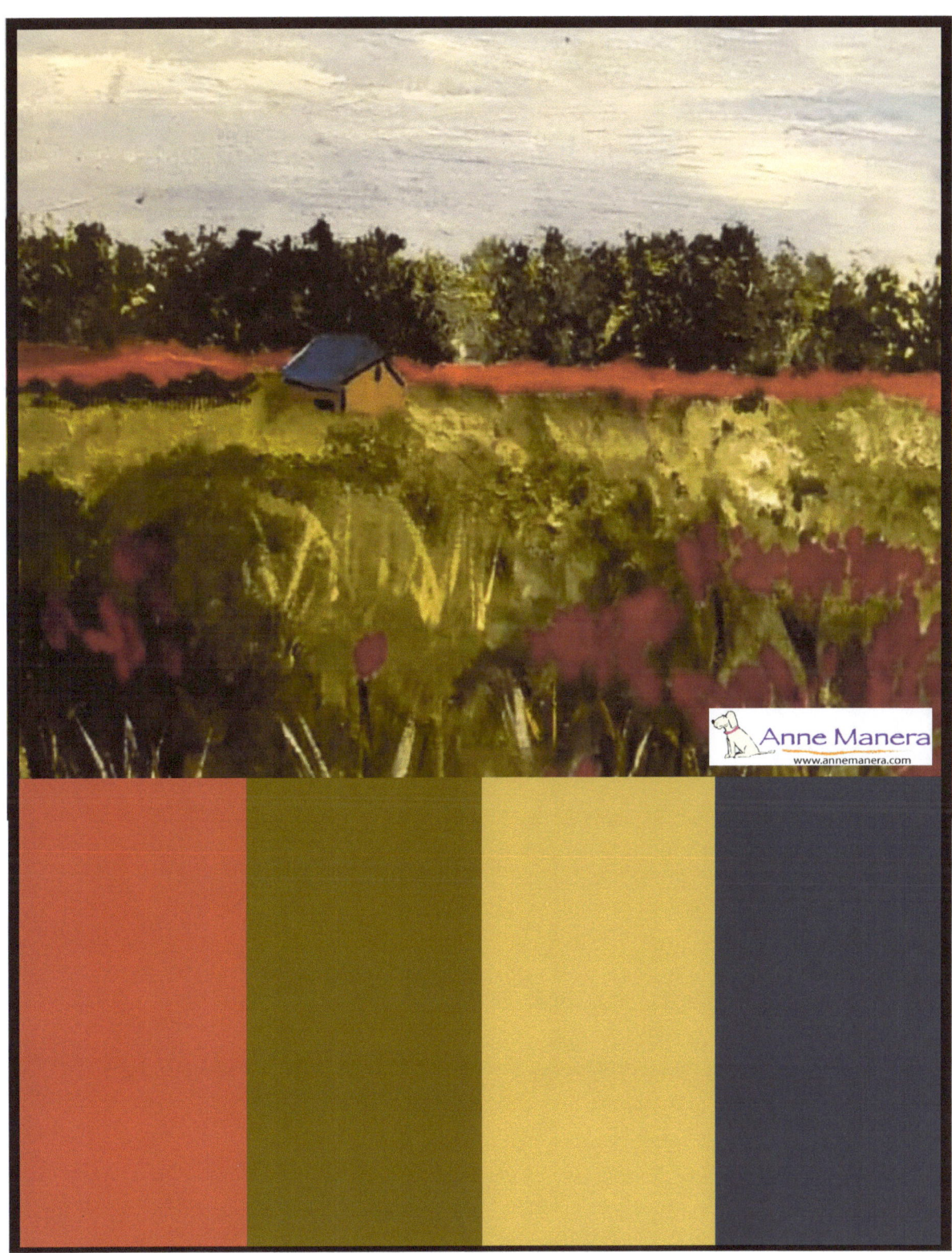

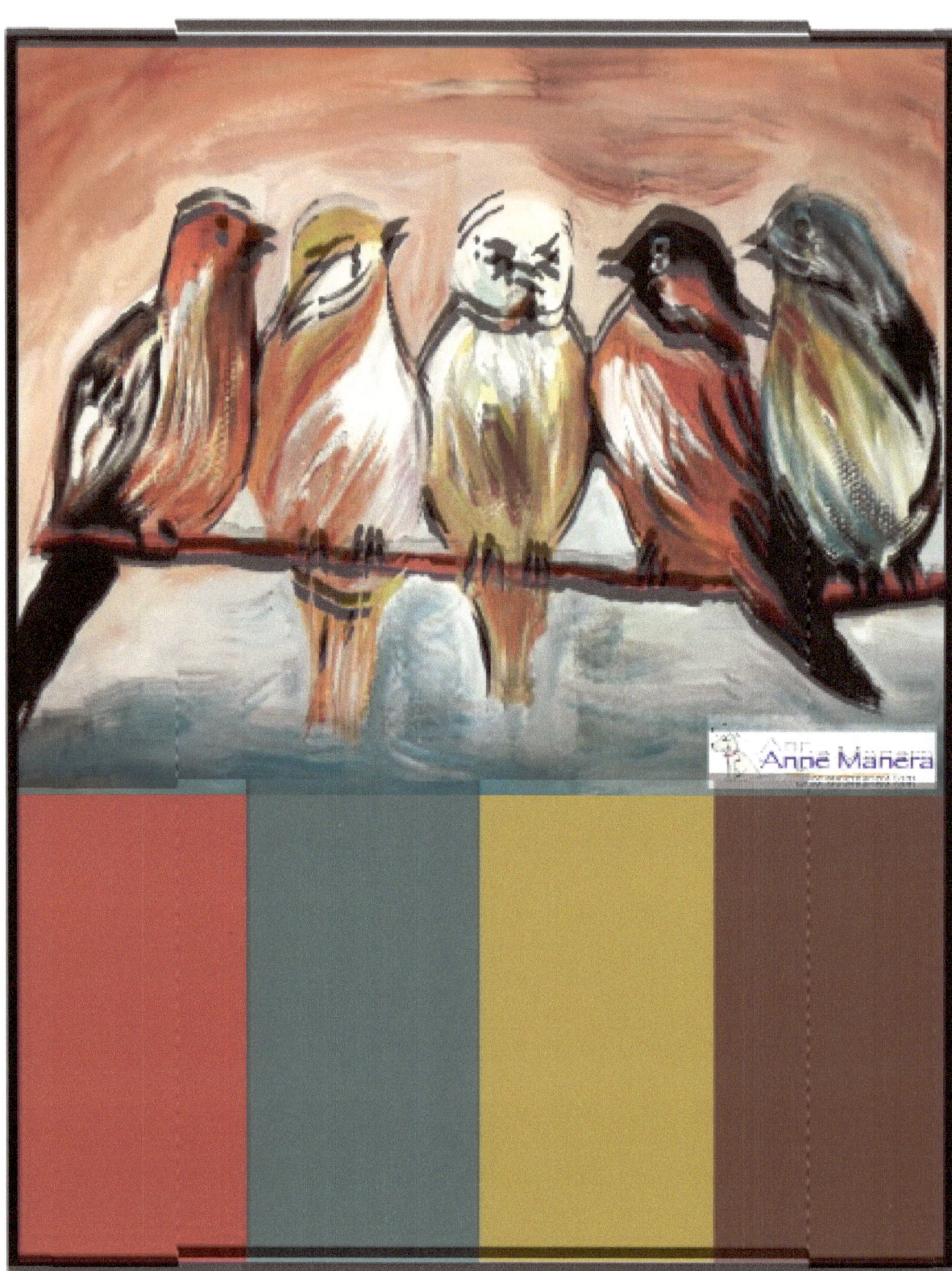

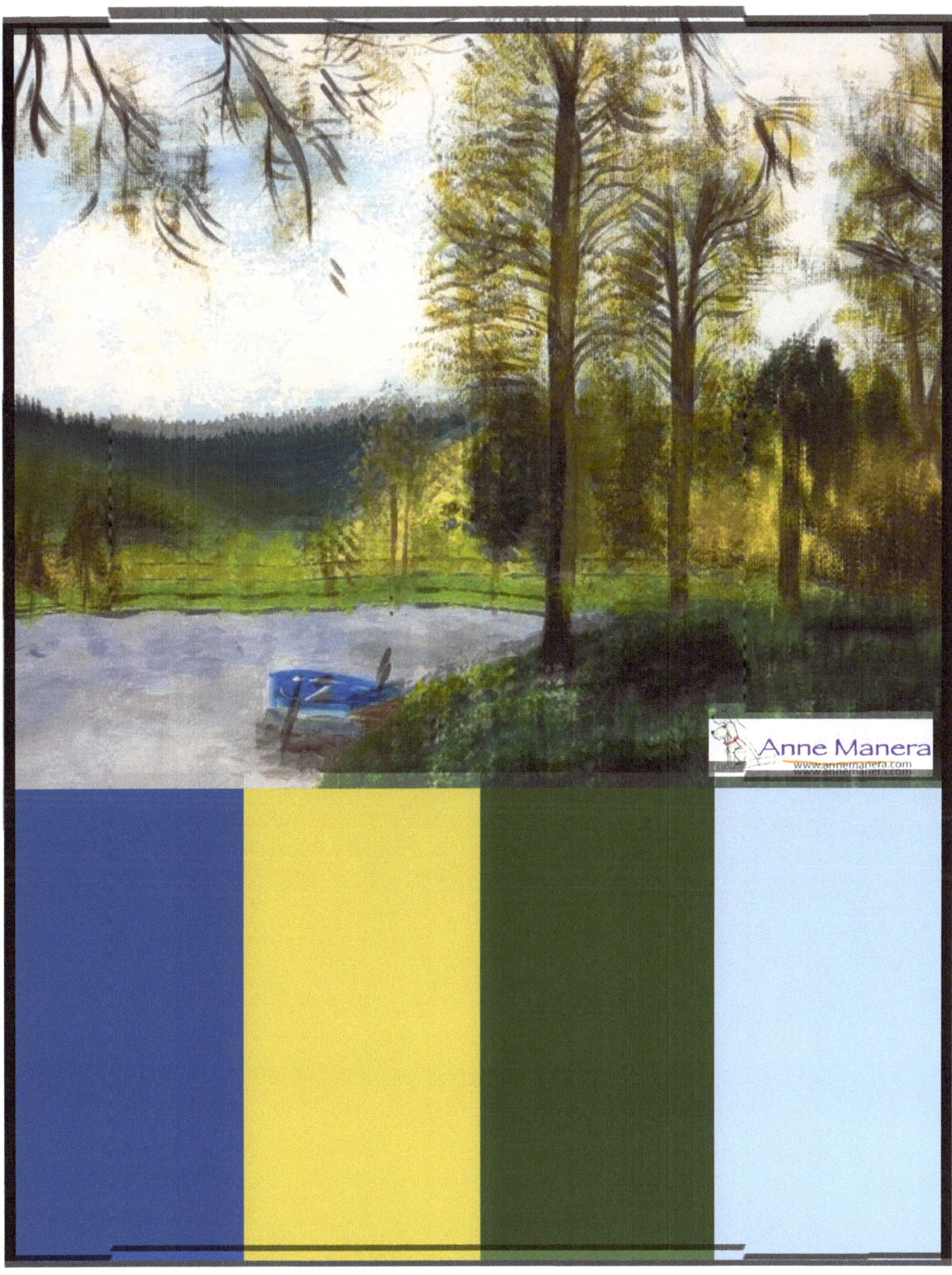

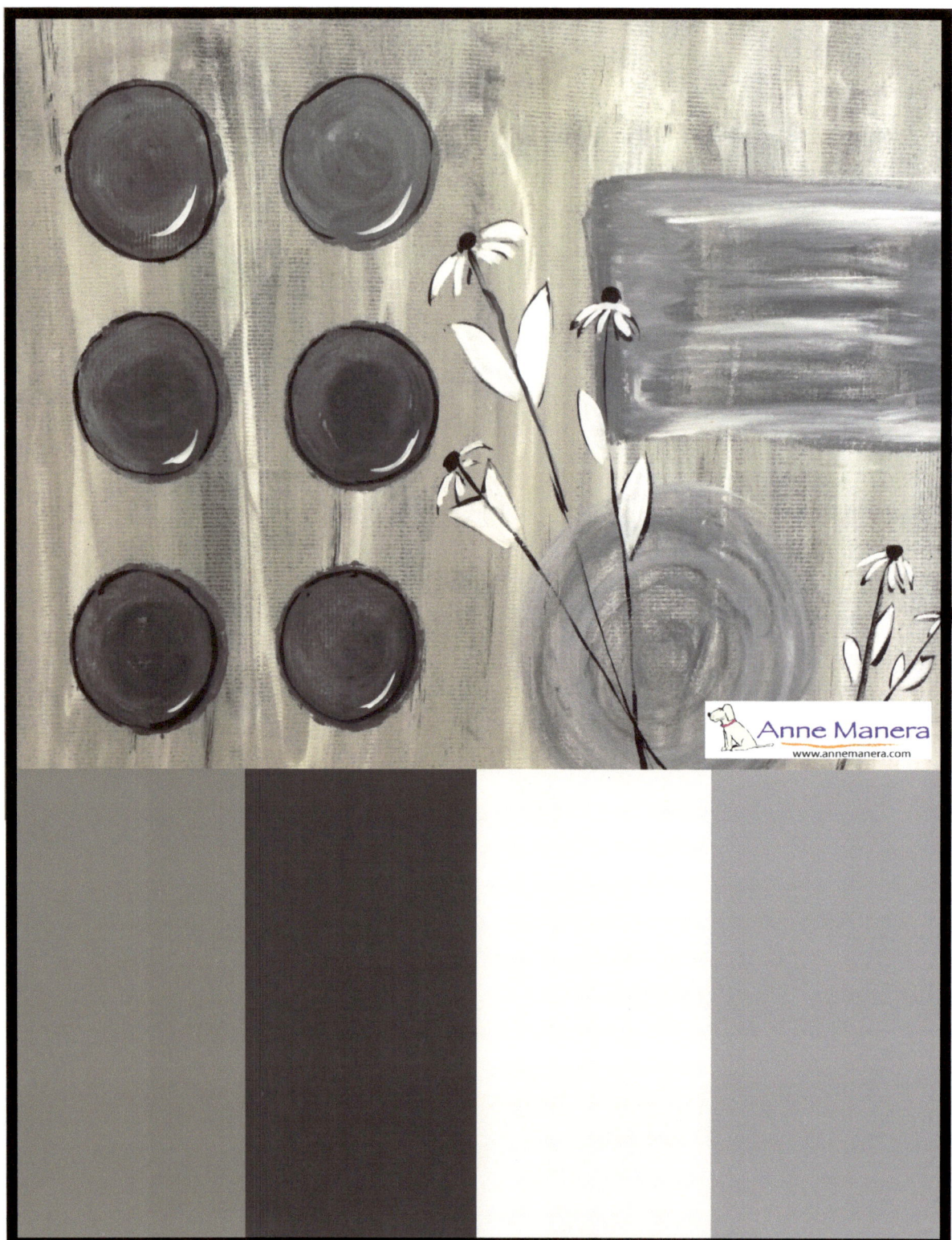

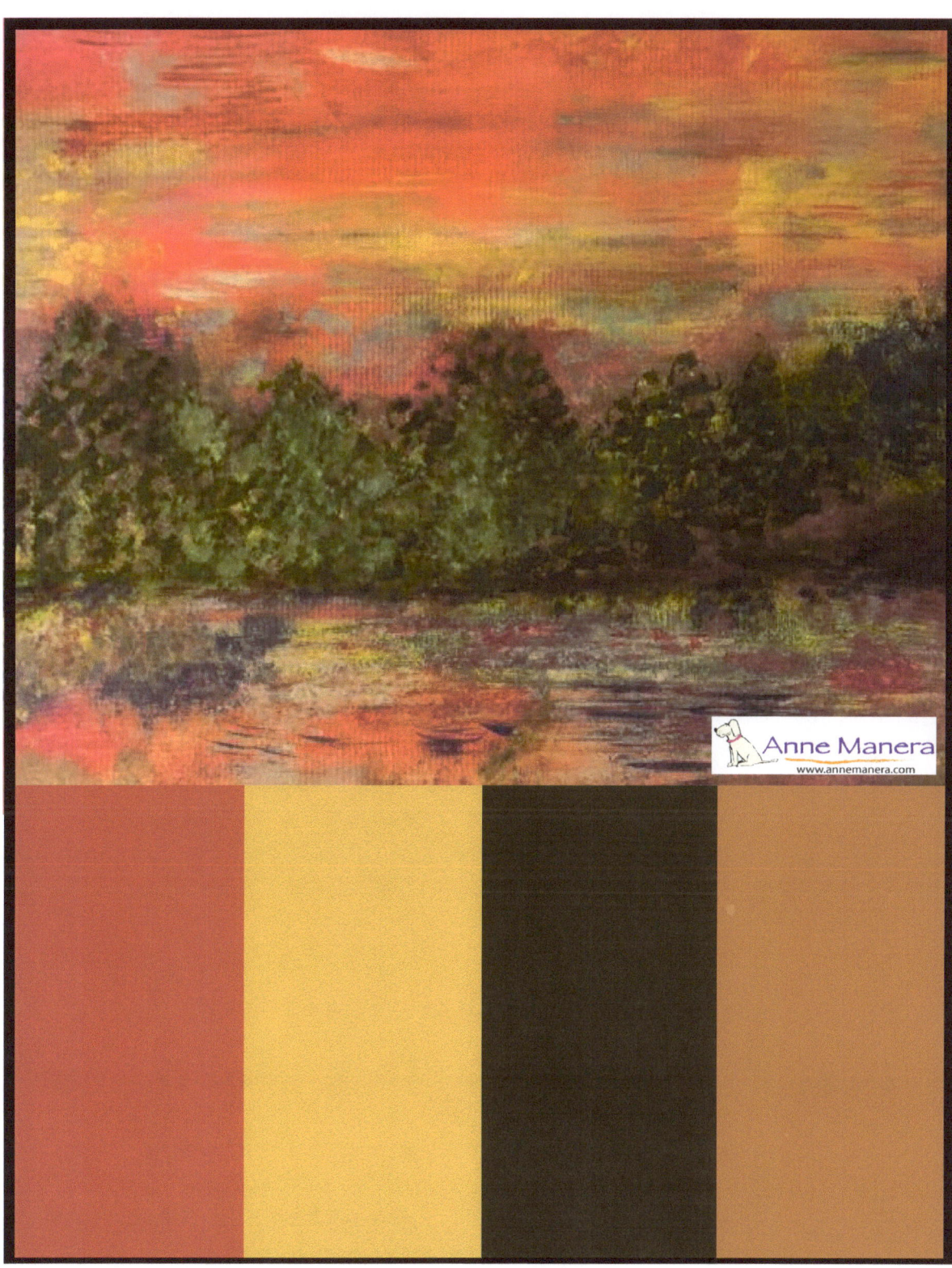

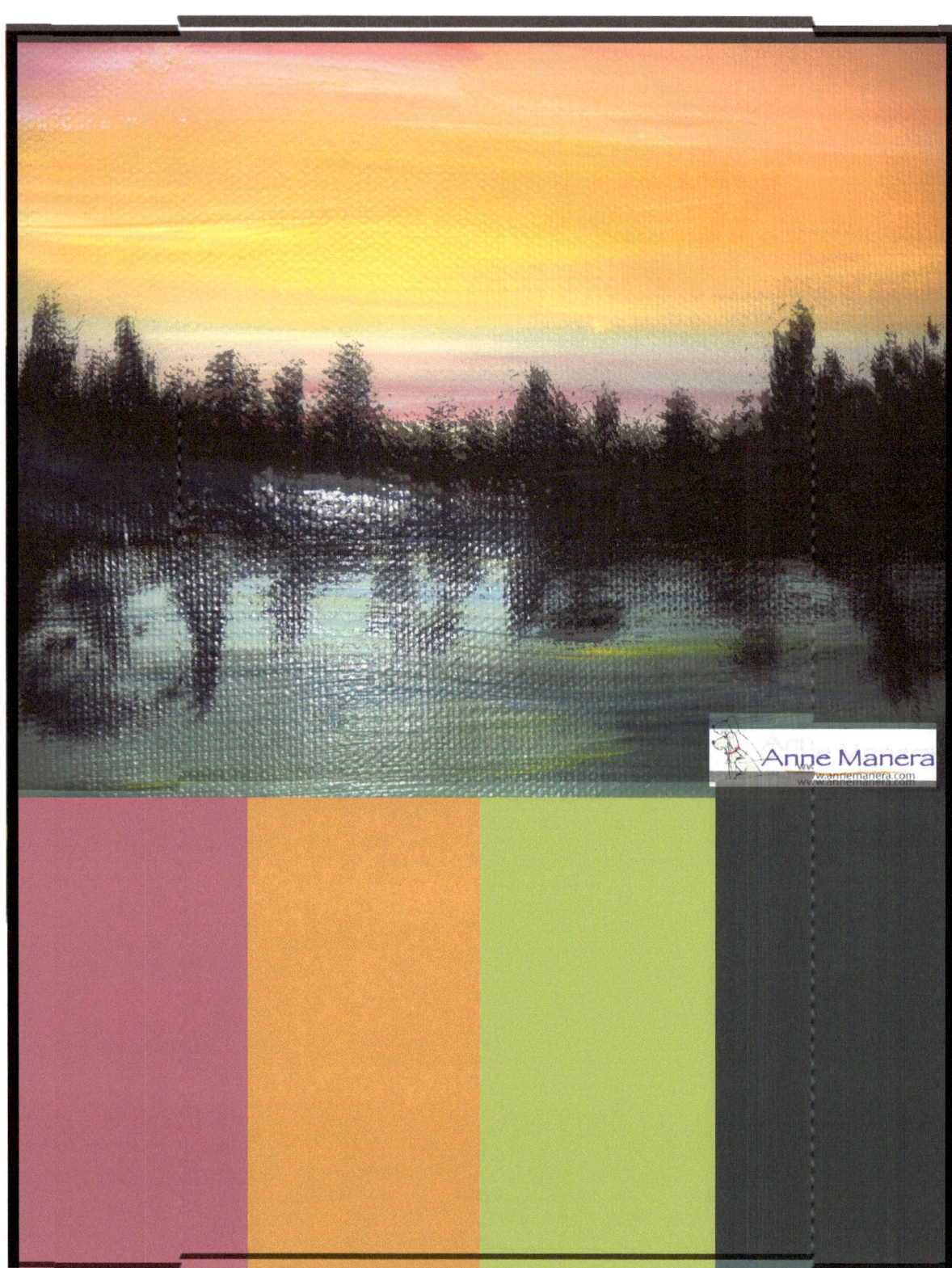

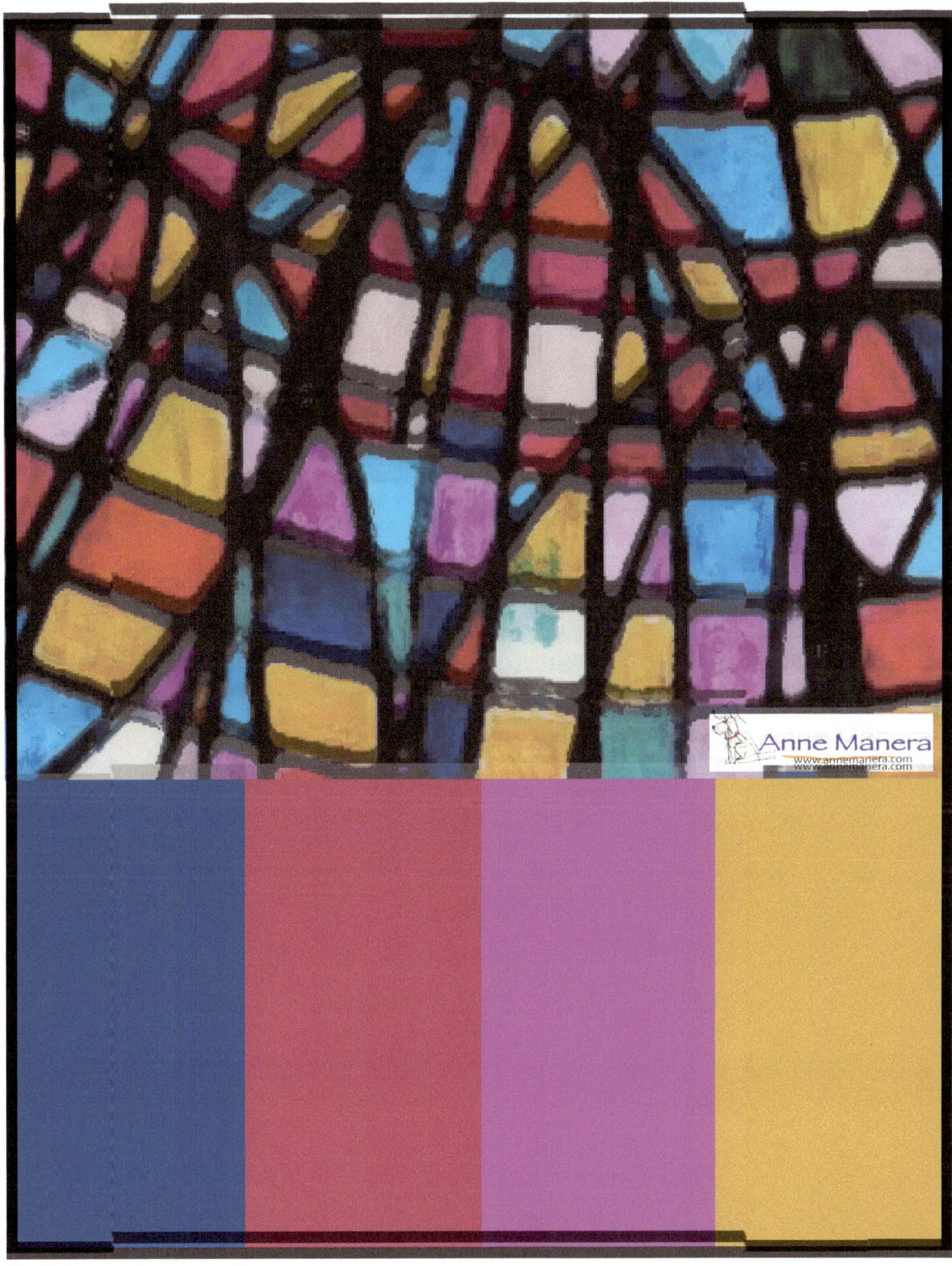

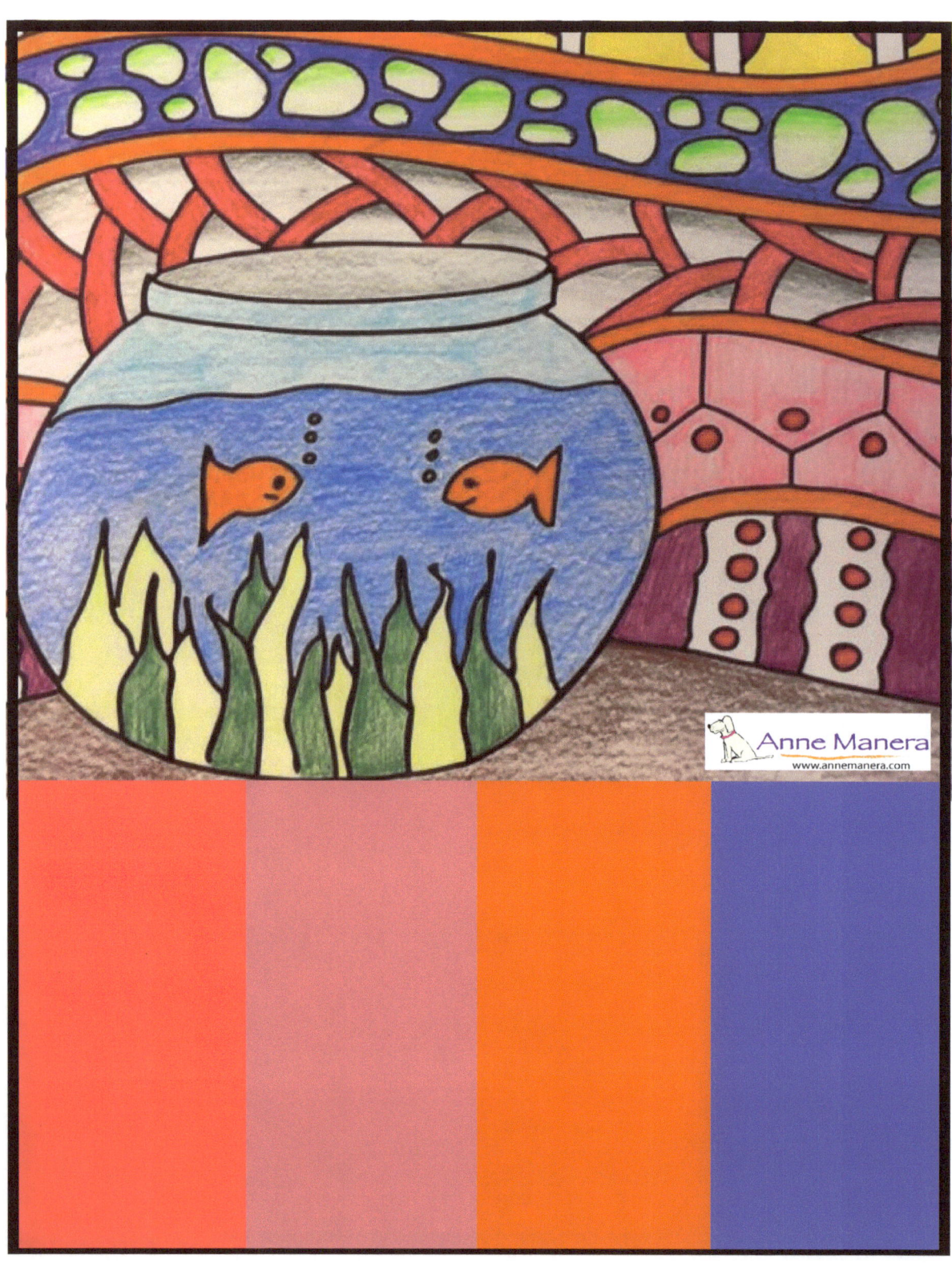

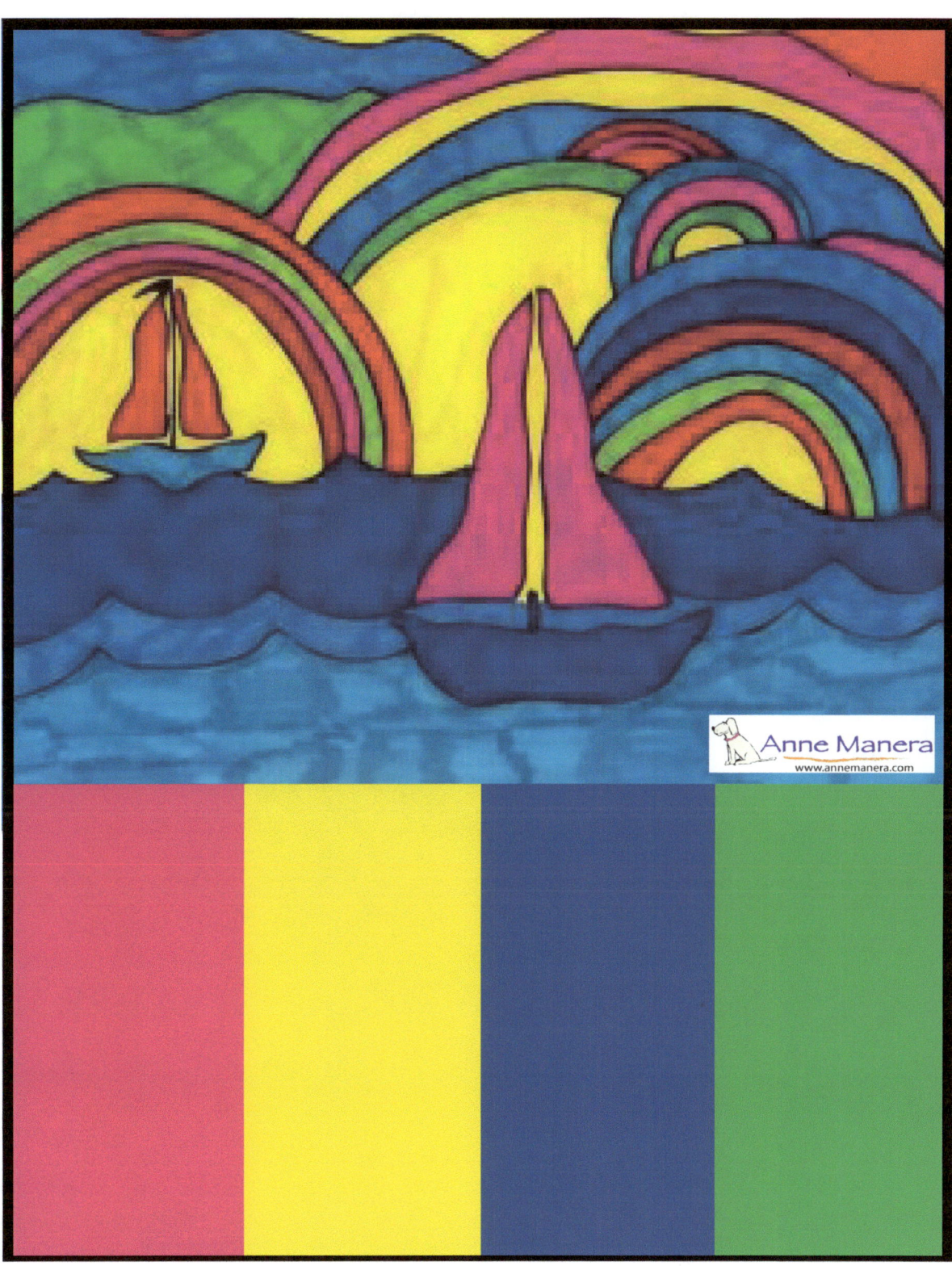

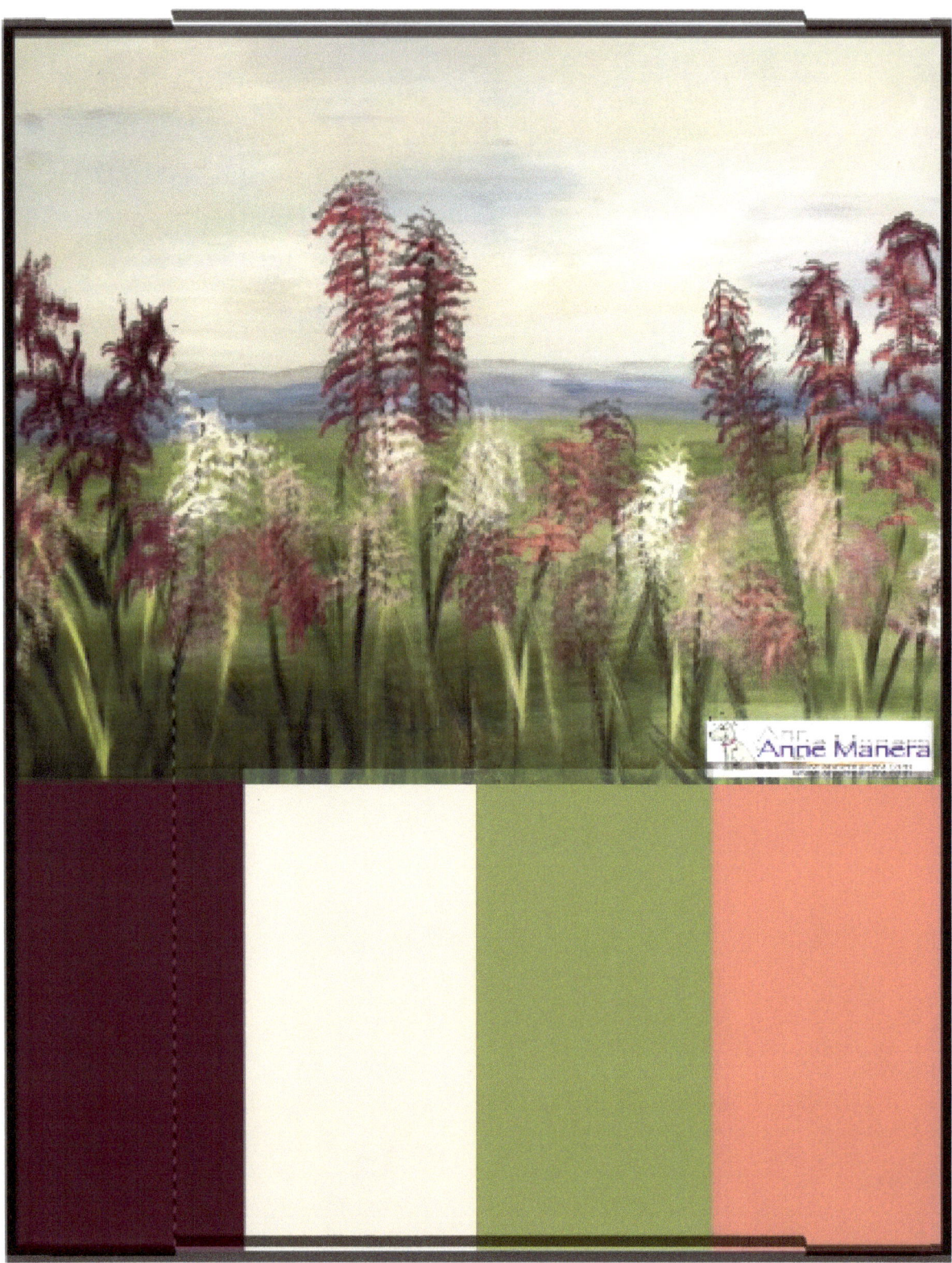

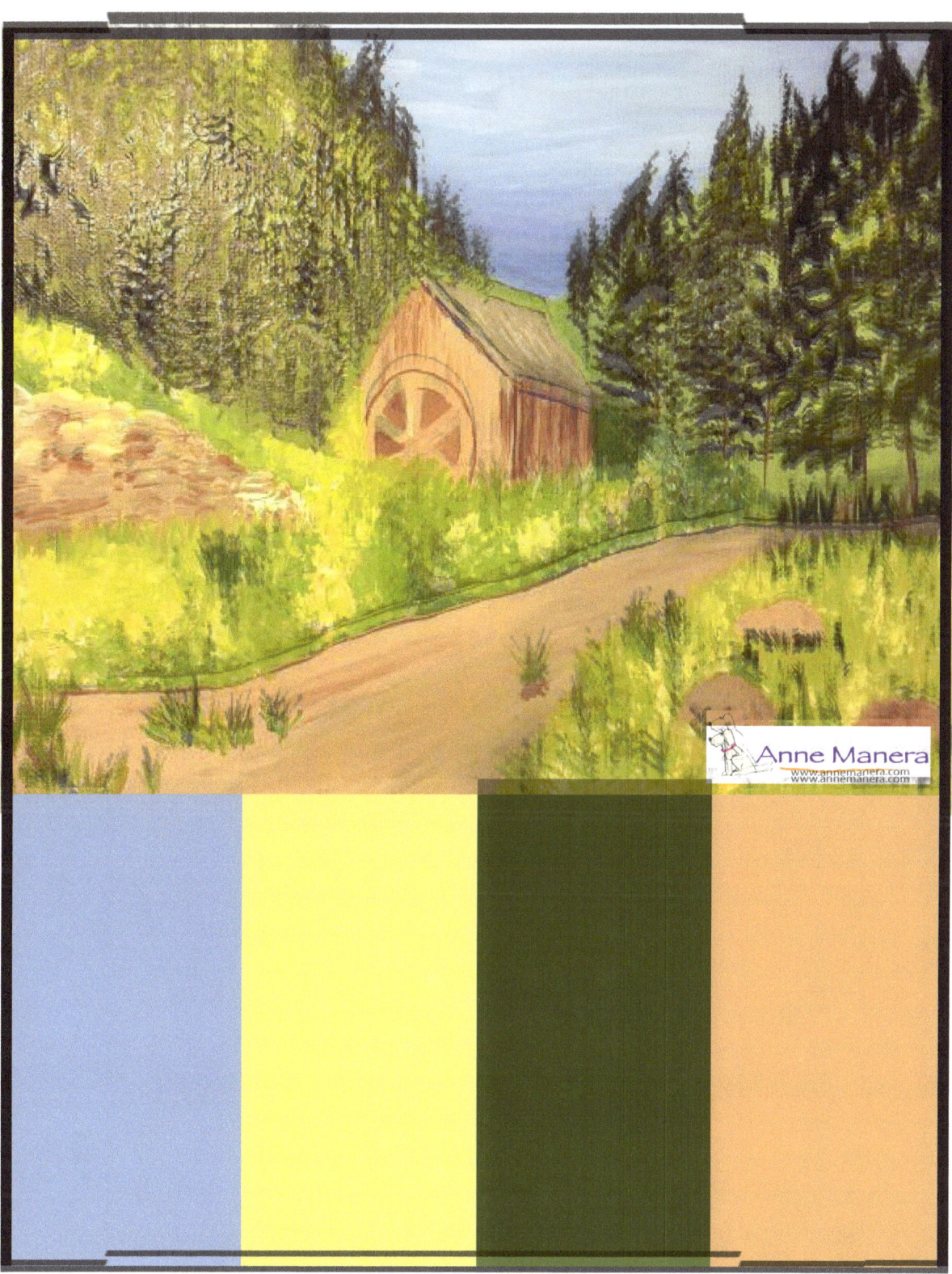

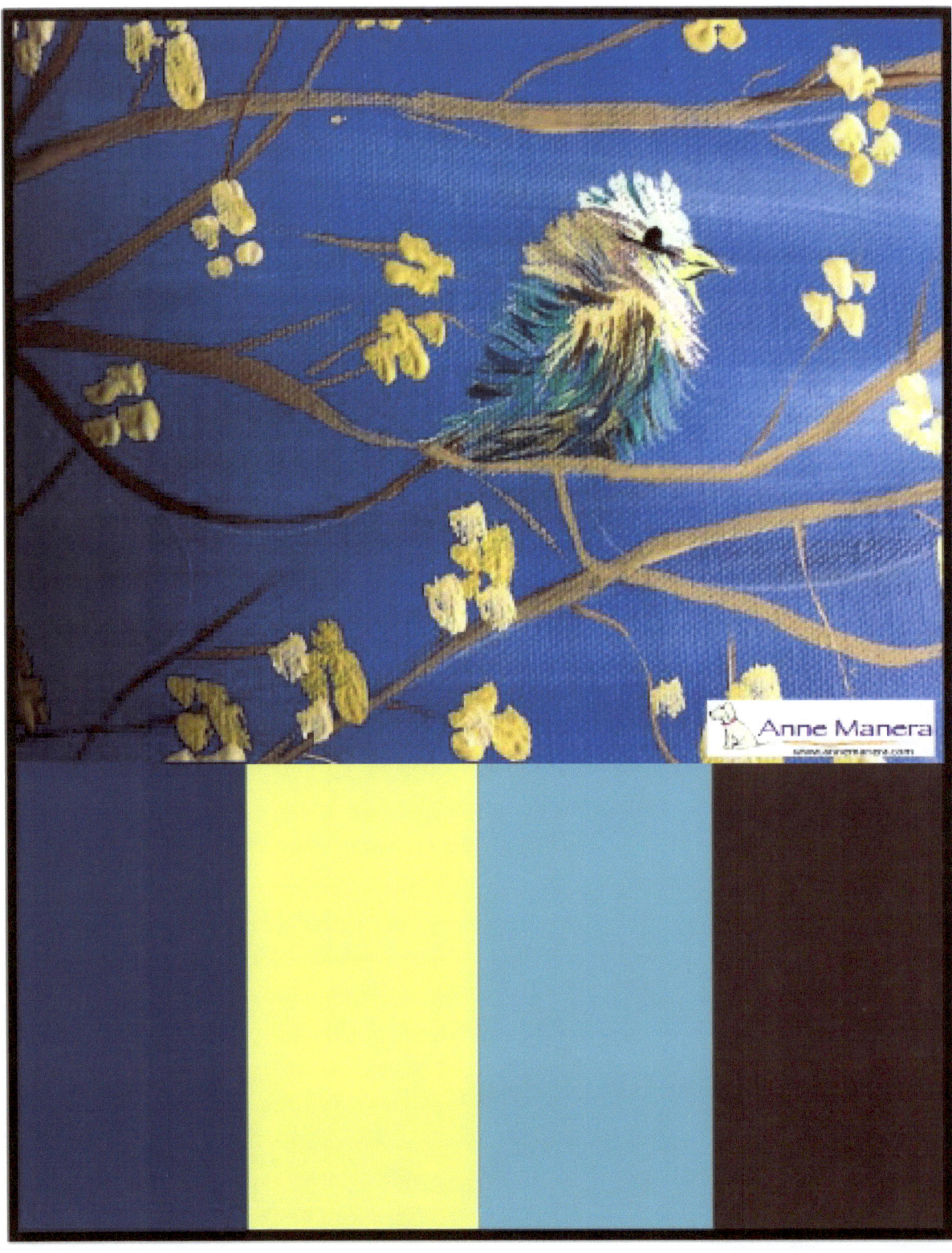

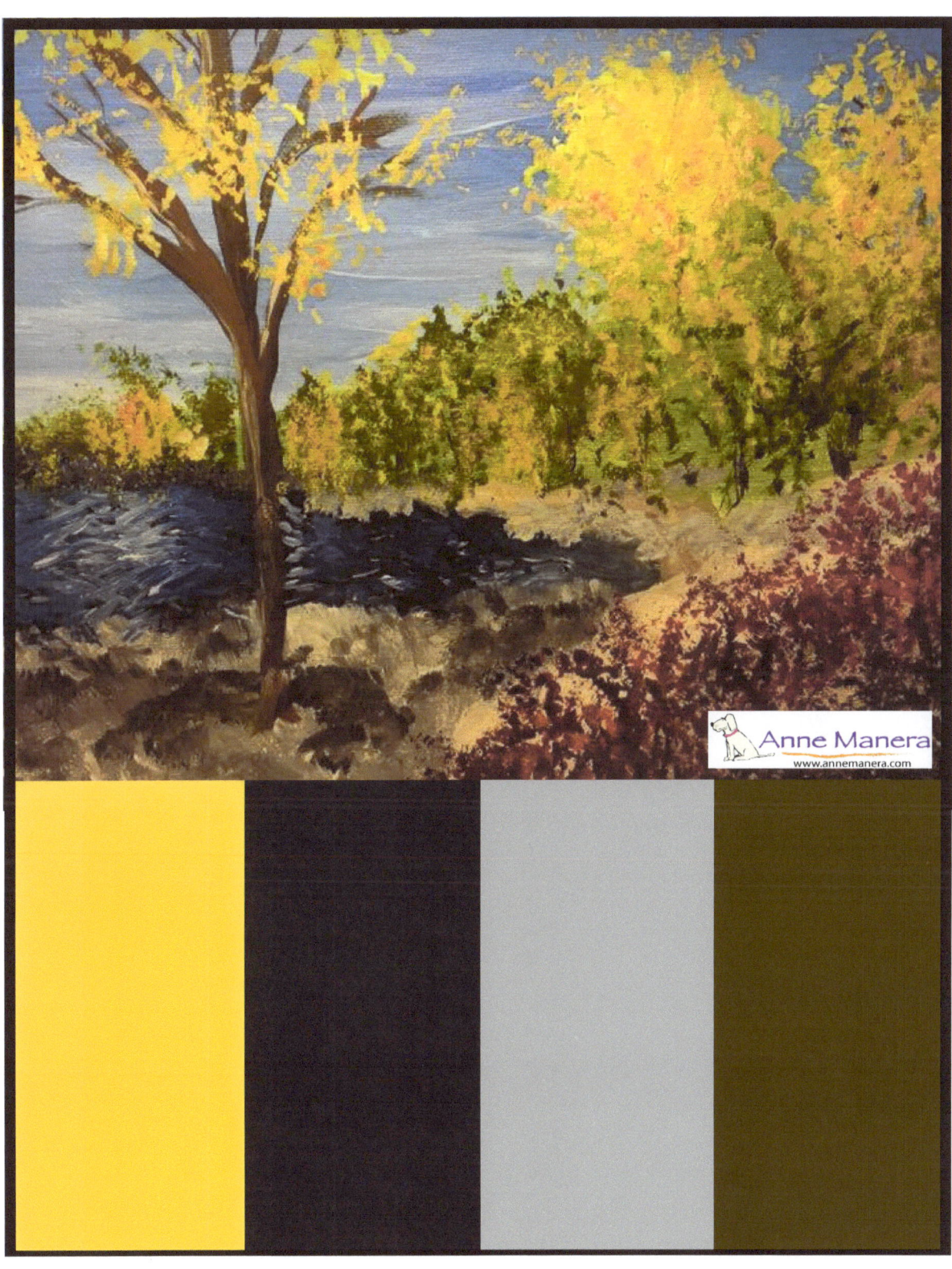

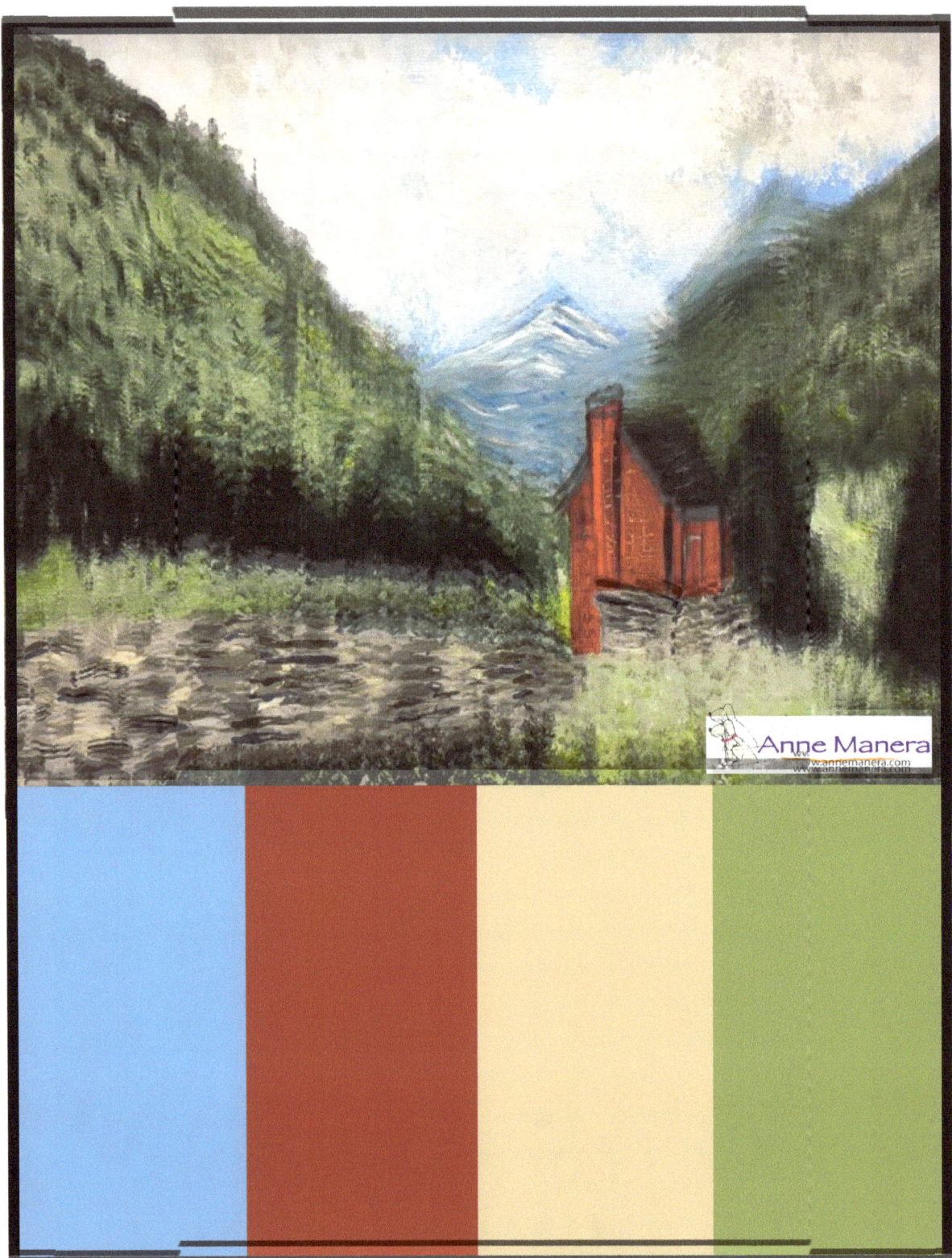

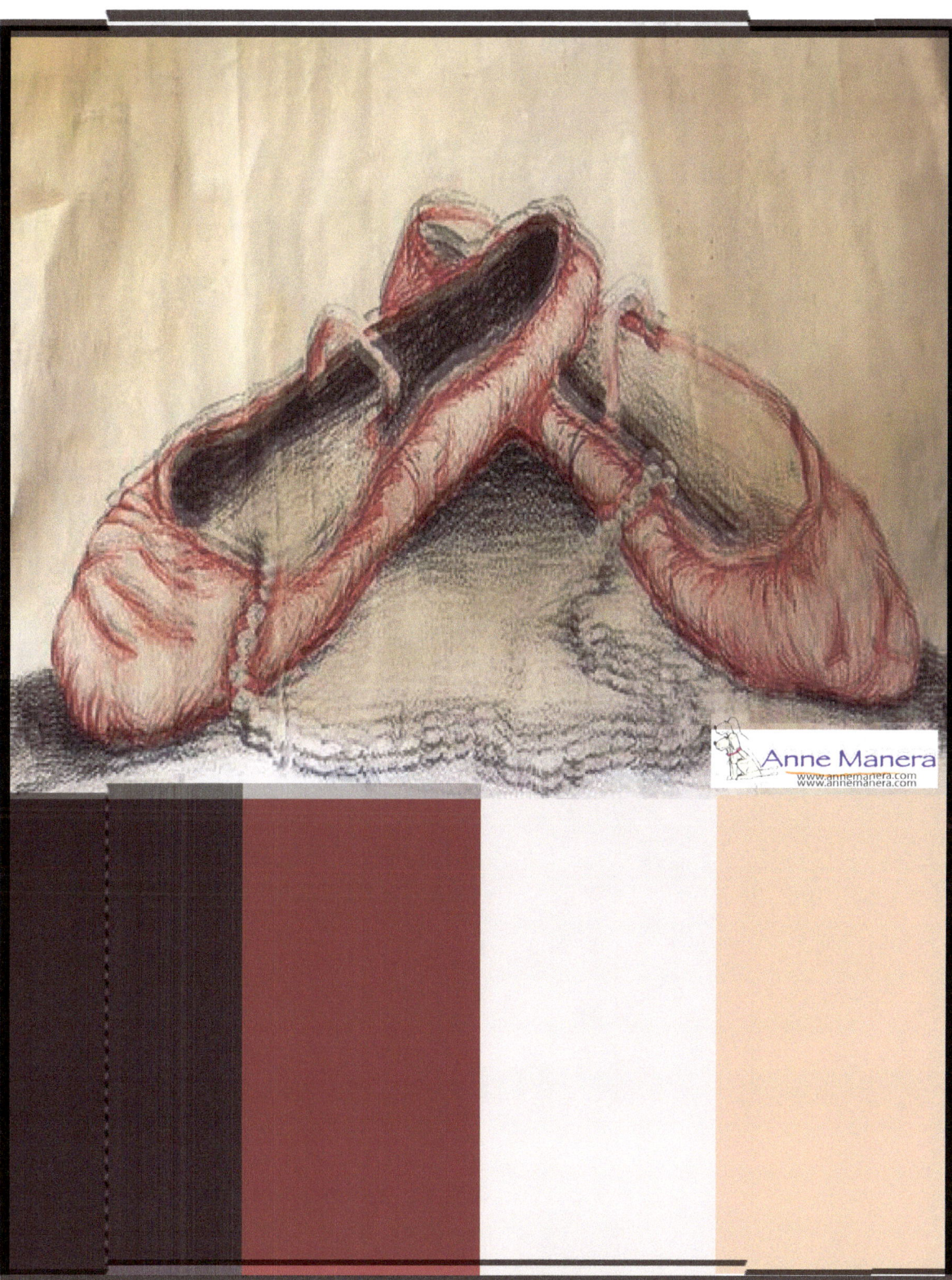

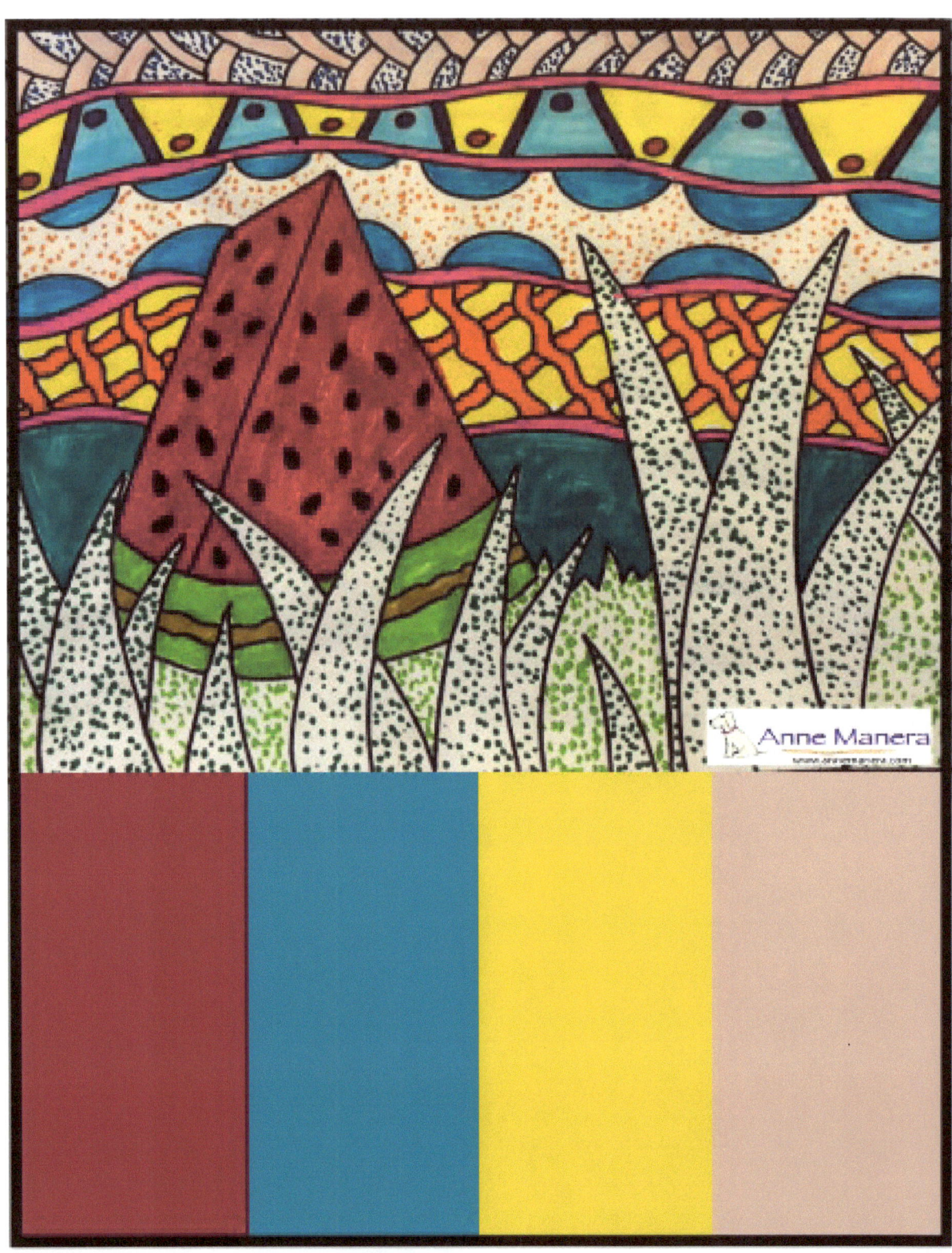

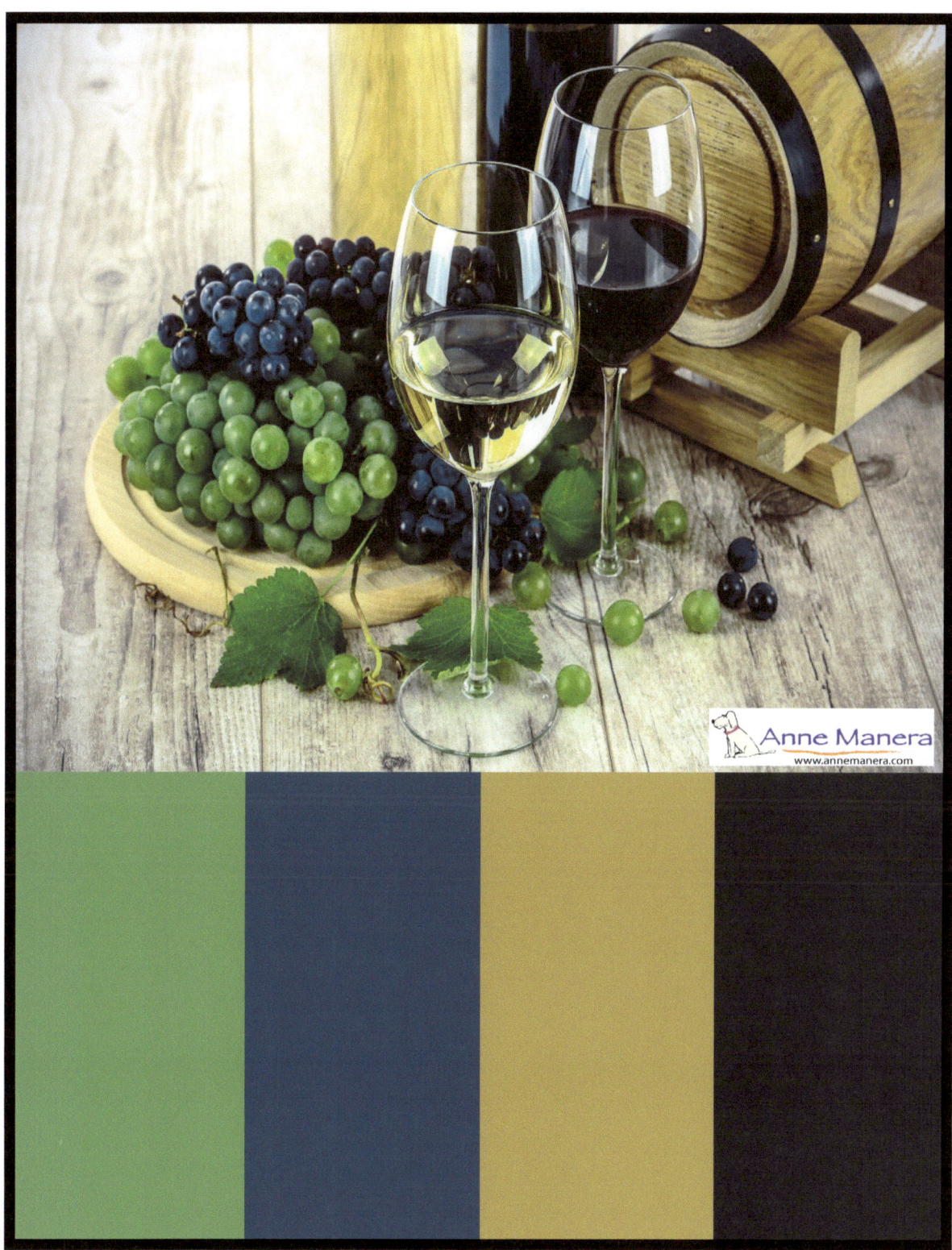

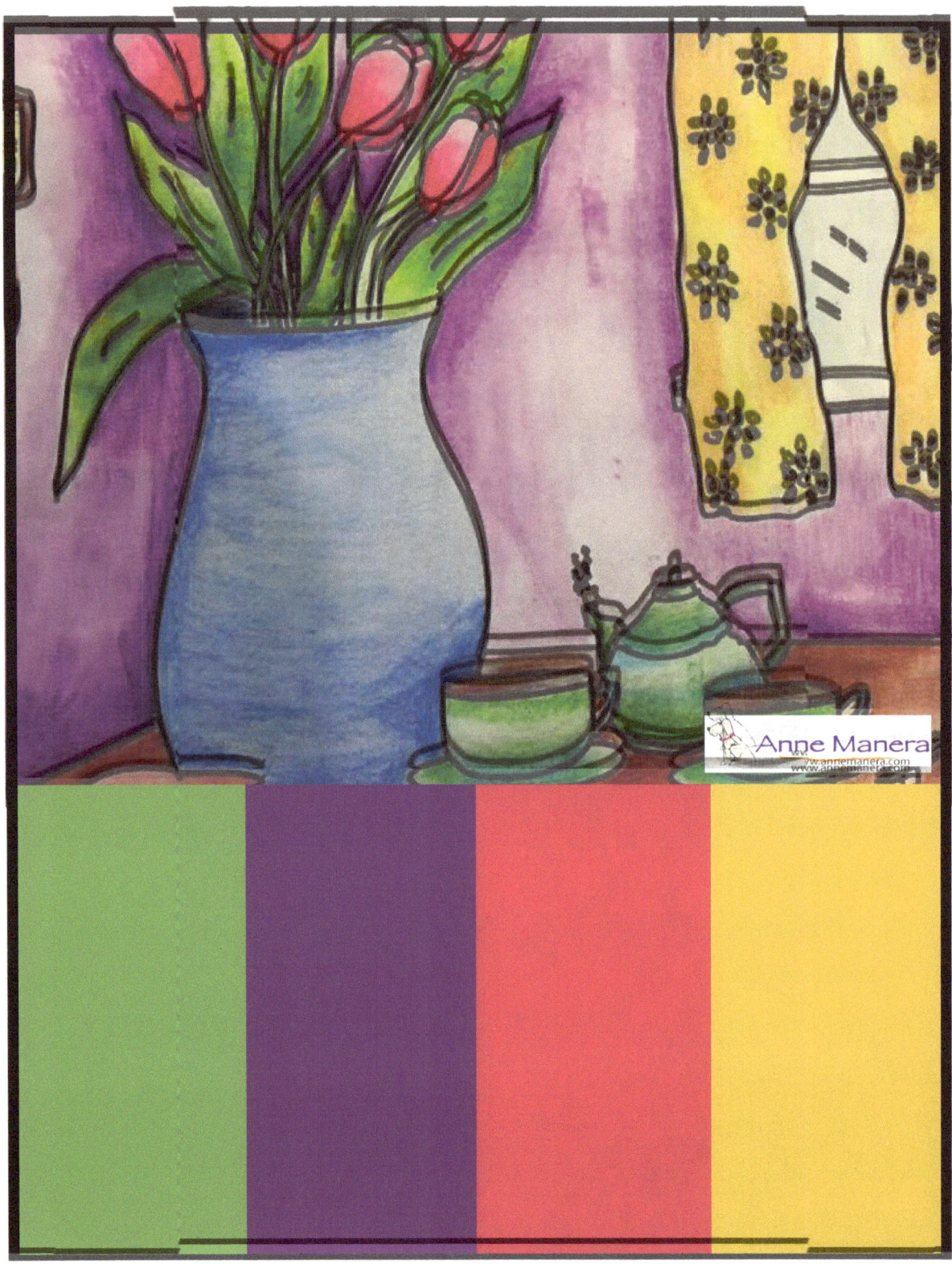

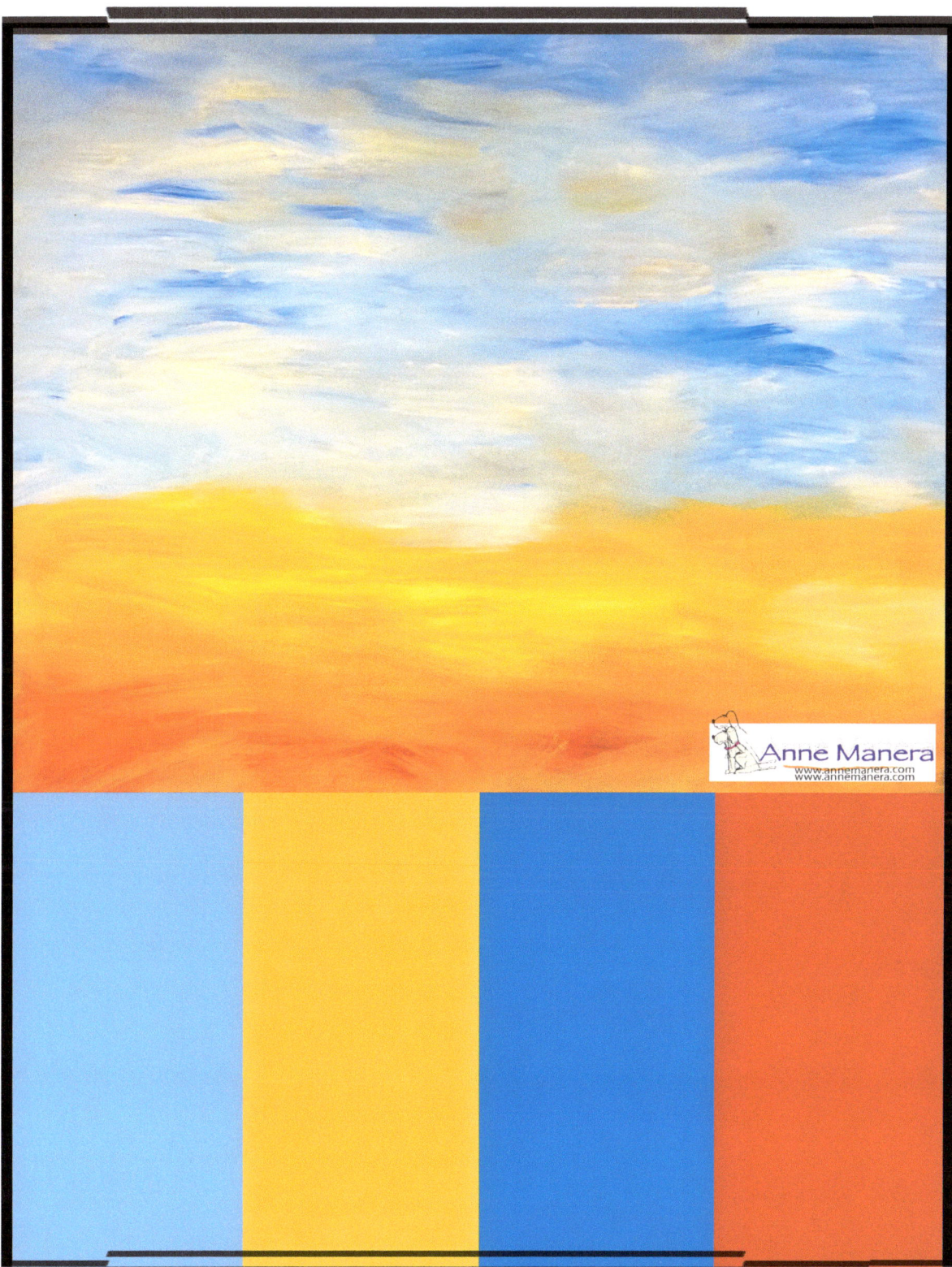

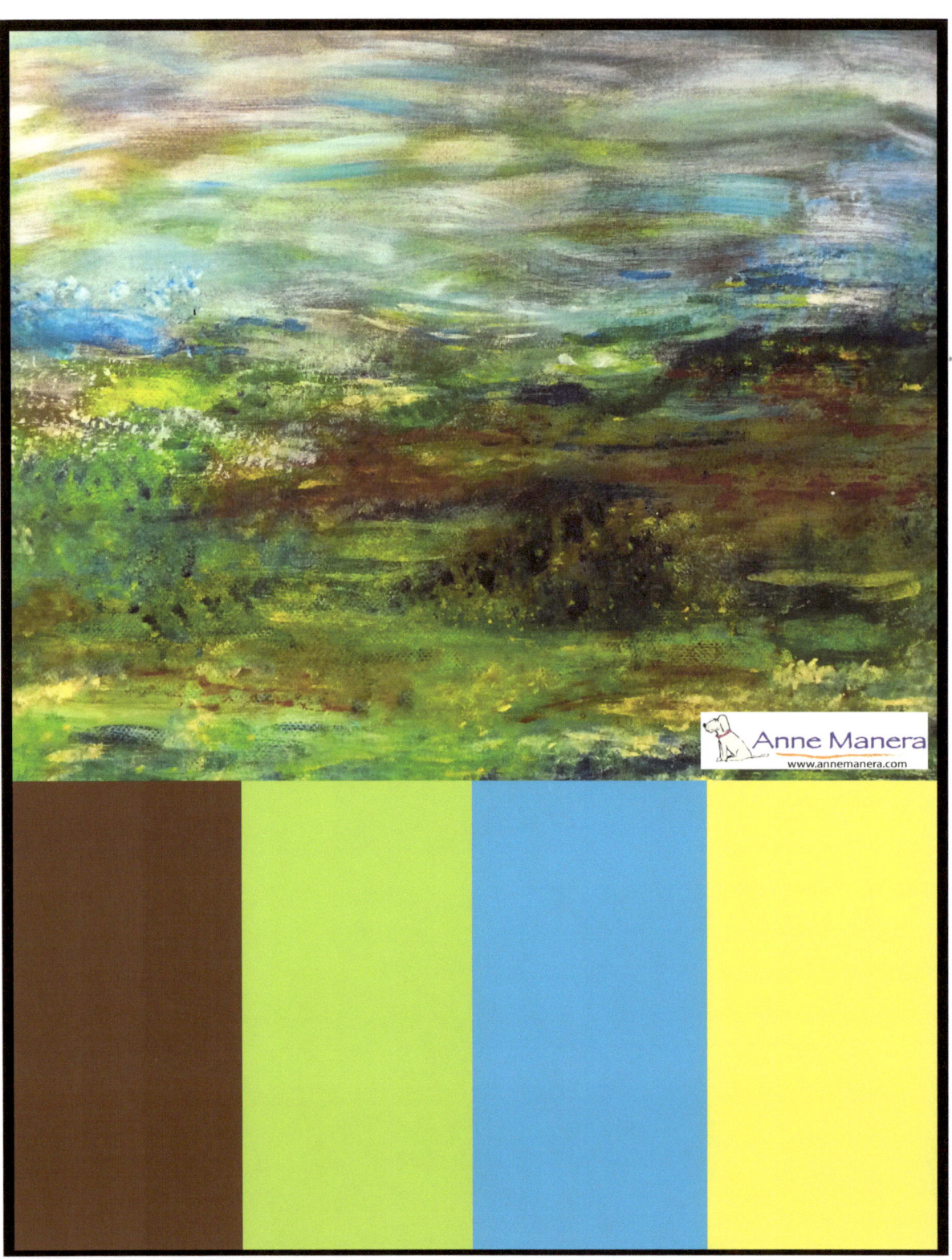

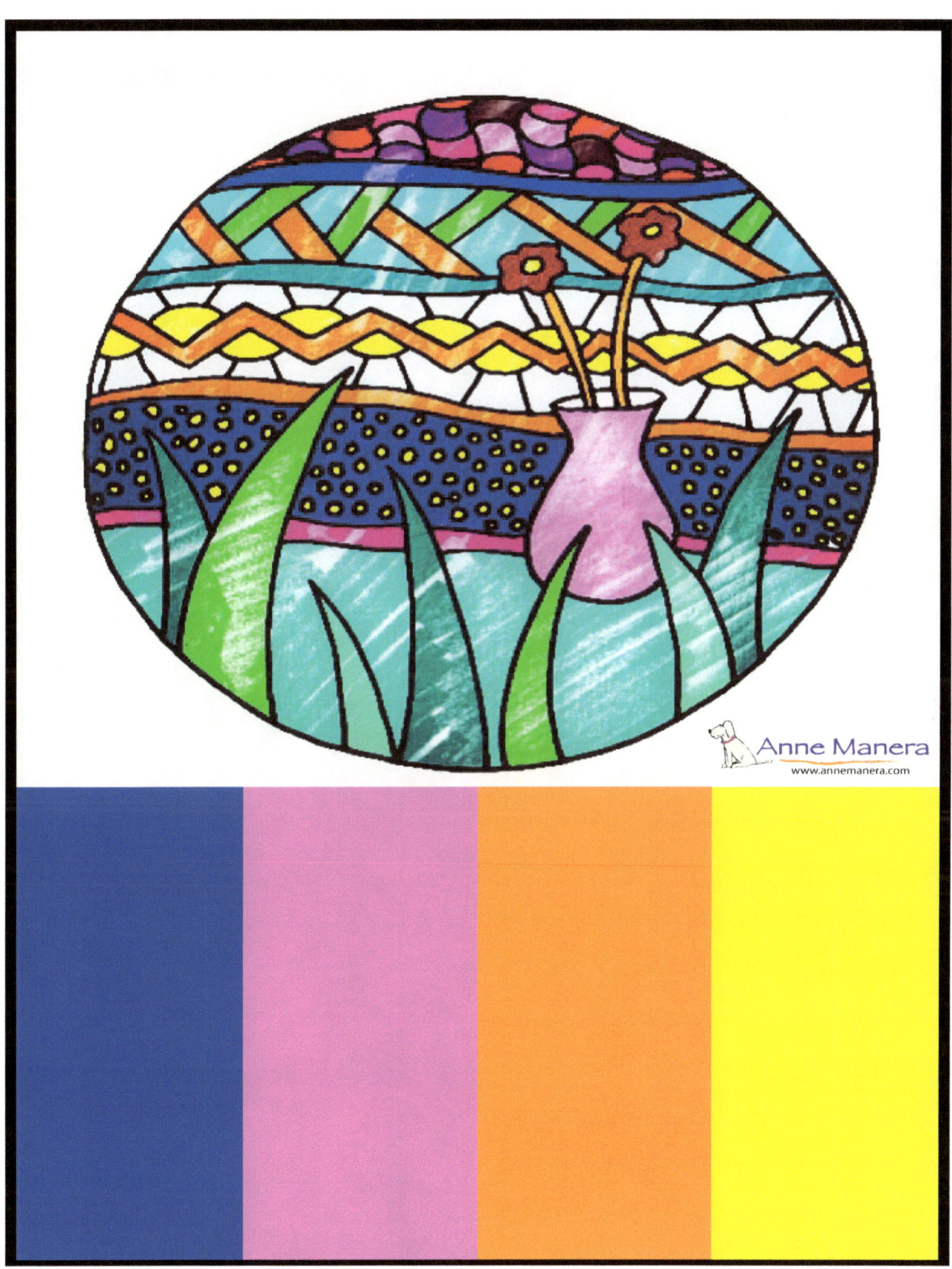

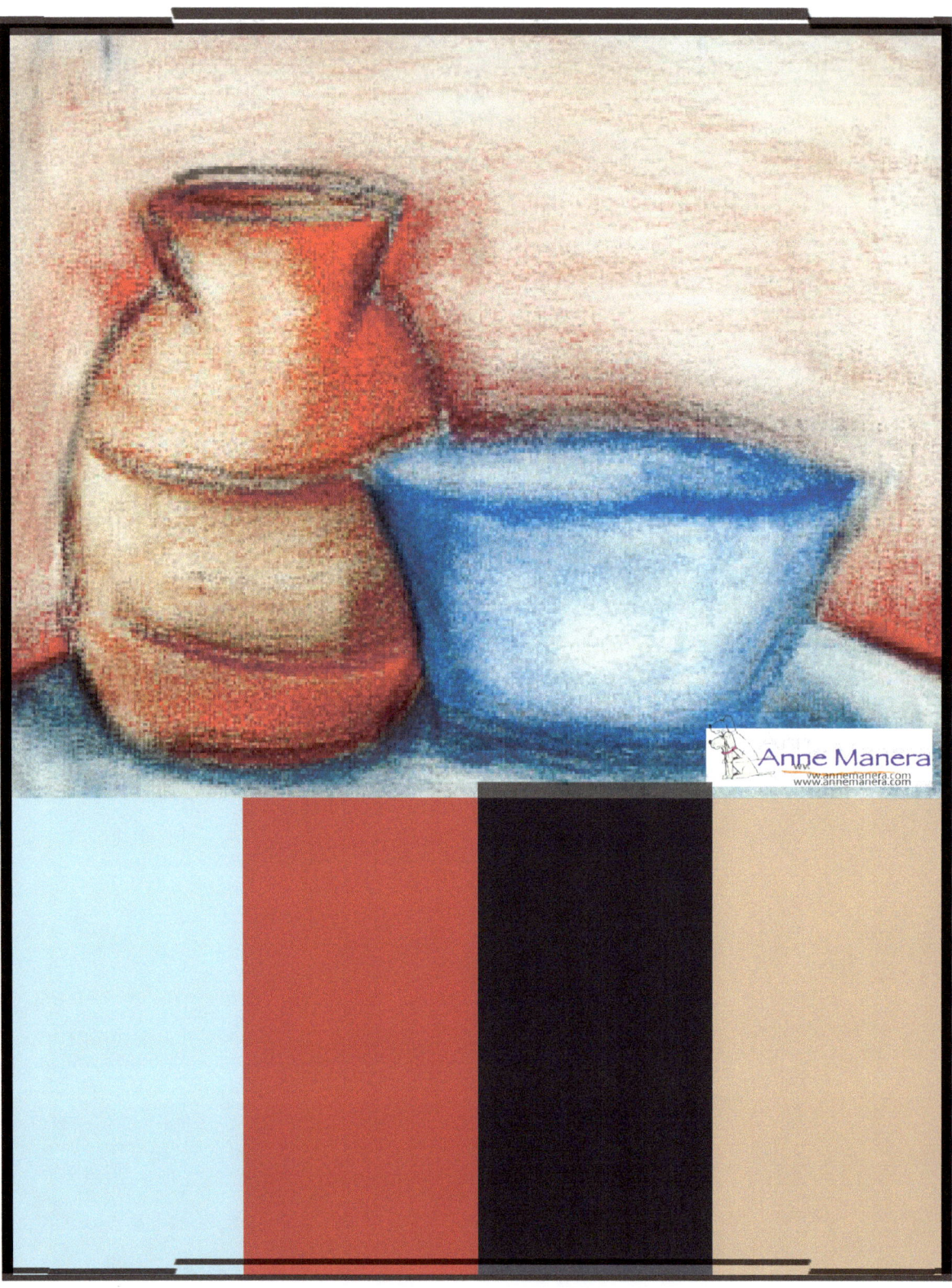

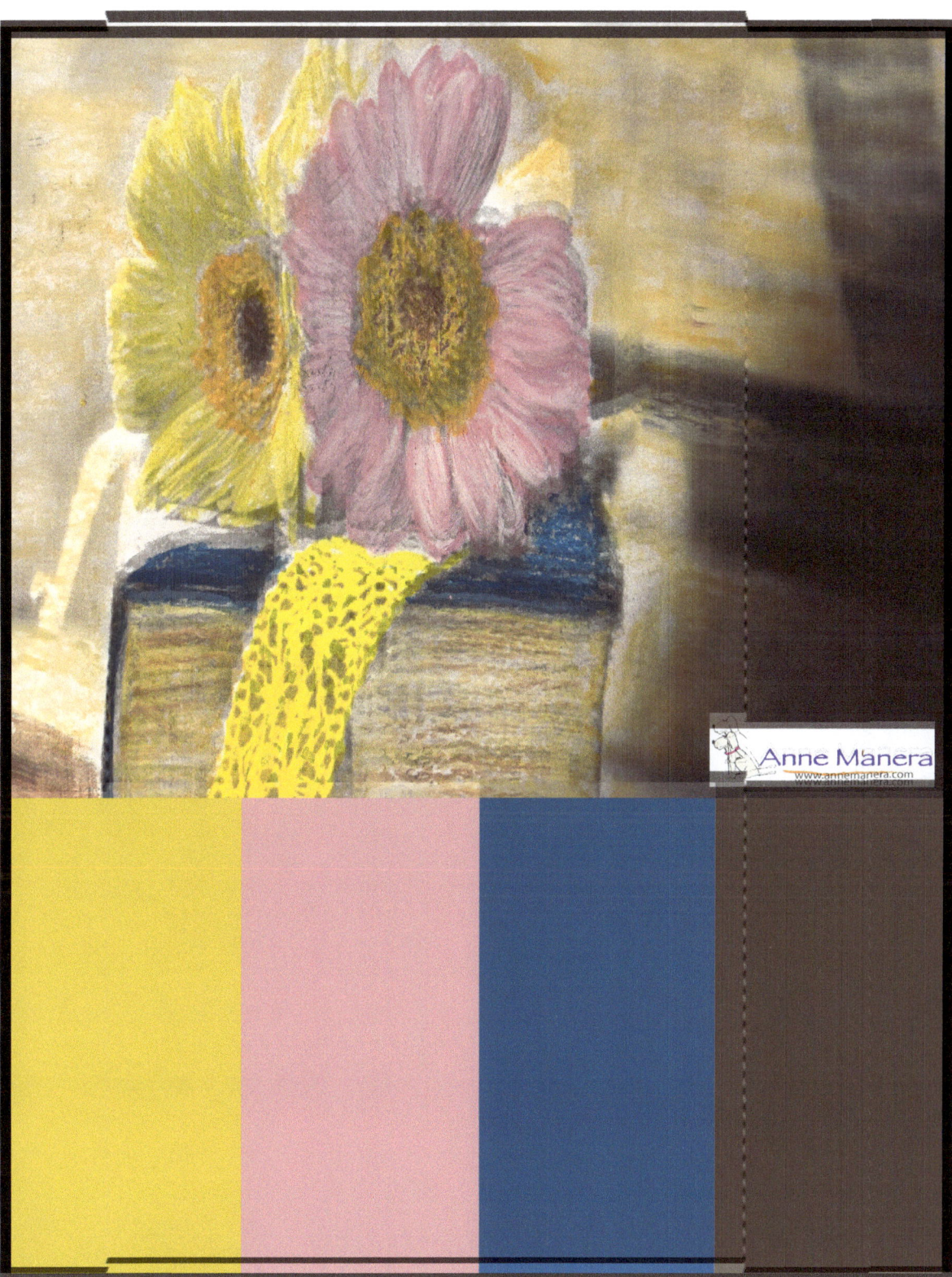

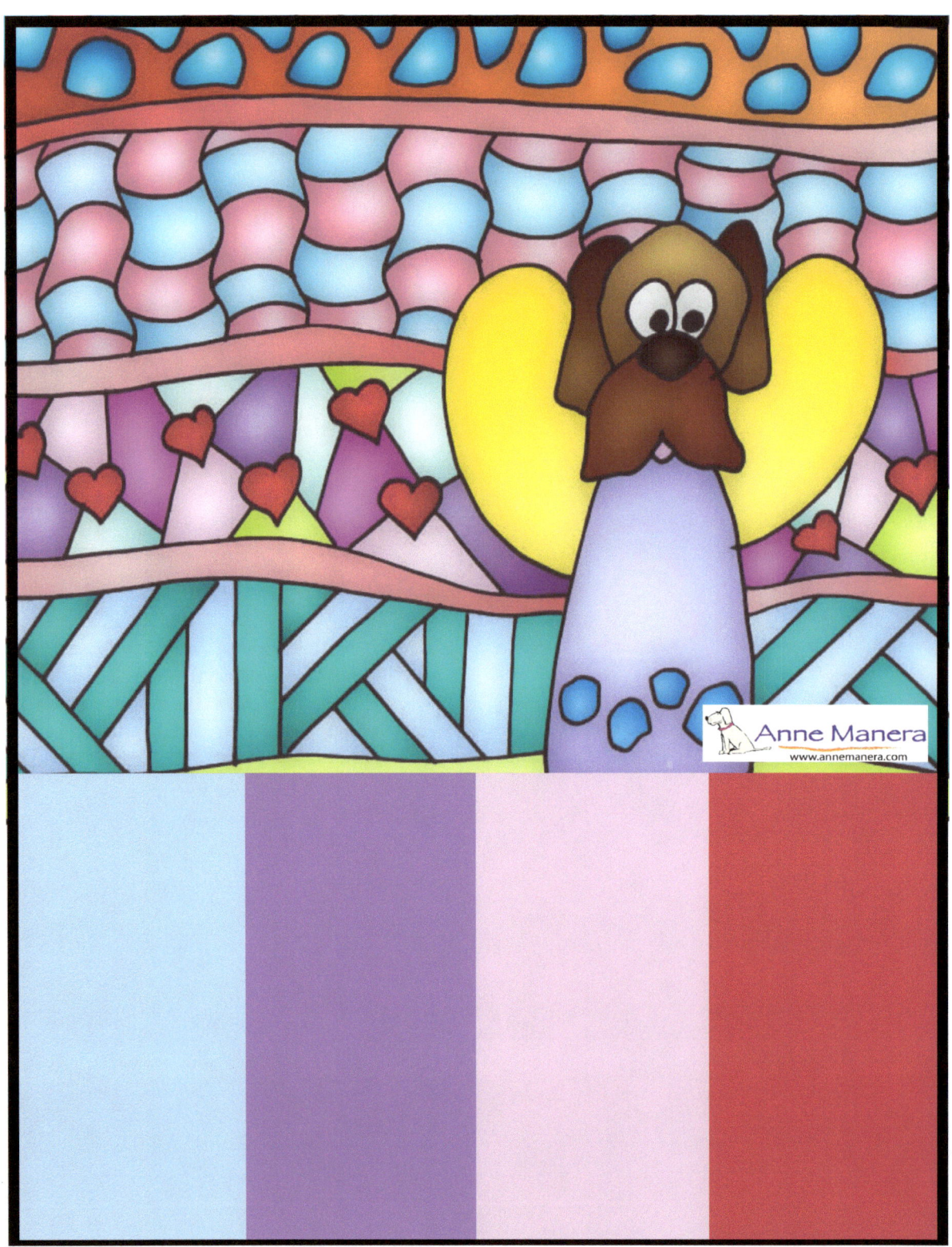

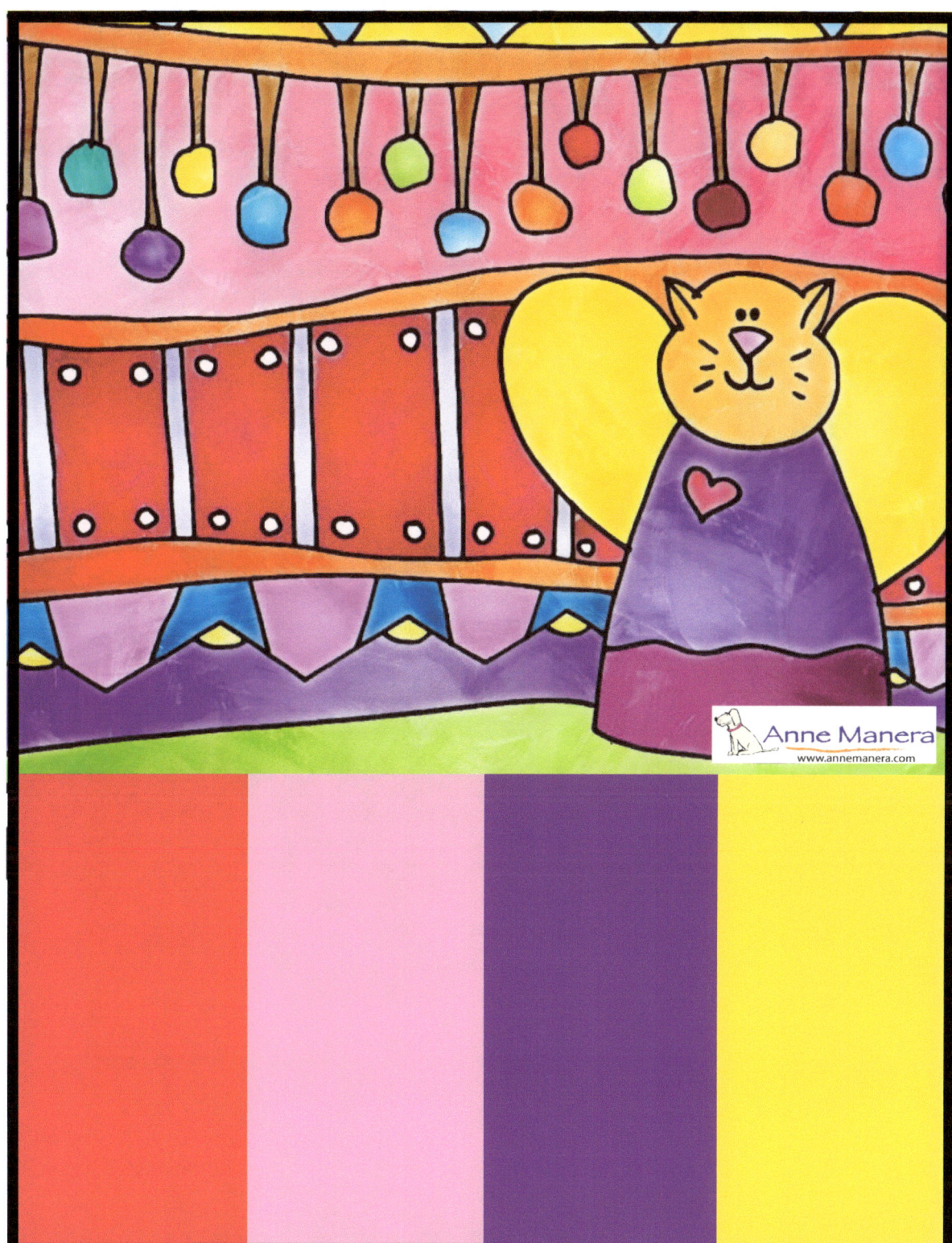

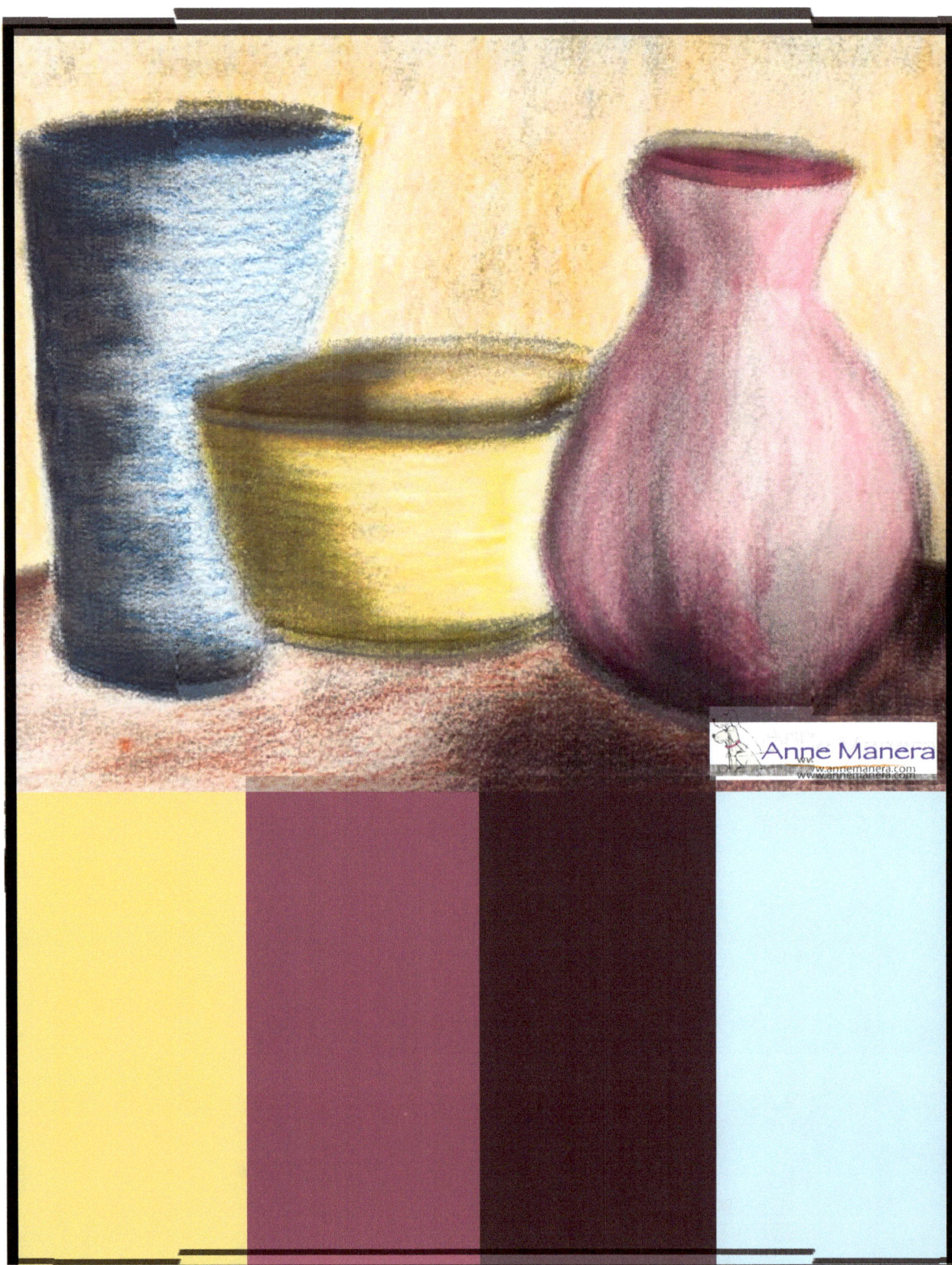

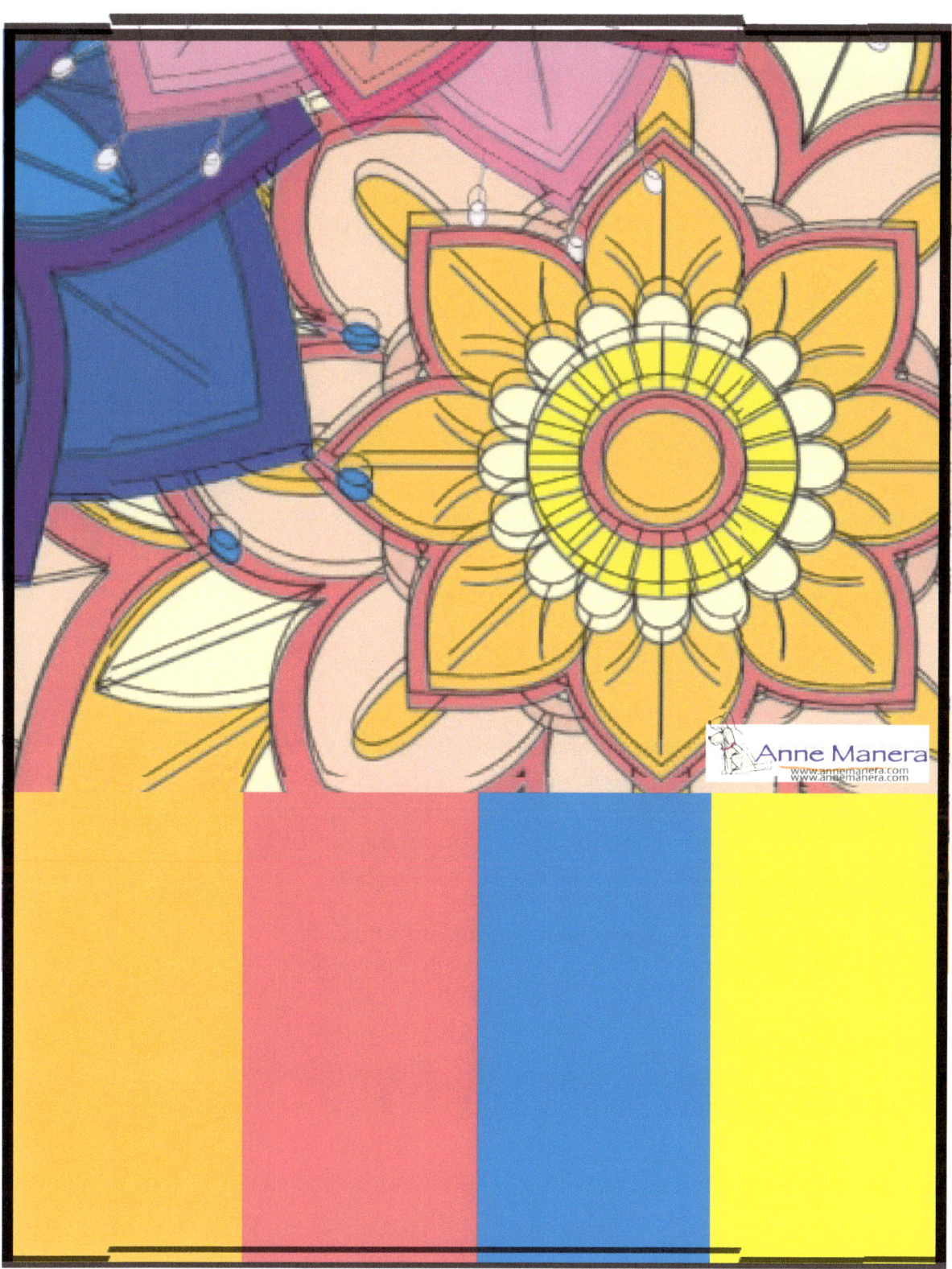

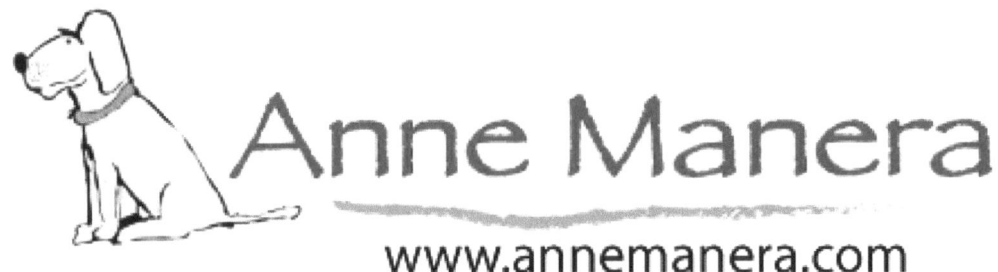

Follow Anne Manera

Amazon Author Page –
www.amazon.com/author/annemanera

Website / Blog –
www.annemanera.com

Facebook –
www.facebook.com/annemanerascoloringbooks

Facebook Coloring Group-
www.facebook.com/groups/coloralongwithannemanera/

Facebook COLOR-ALONG Coloring Group –
www.facebook.com/groups/JustColorGroup

Twitter –
www.twitter.com/annemanera

Instagram –
www.instagram.com/anne.manera